Contemporary Issues
in Special Education

Contemporary Issues in Special Education

First Edition

Ashlea L. Rineer-Hershey and Toni Mild

cognella®
SAN DIEGO

Bassim Hamadeh, CEO and Publisher
John Remington, Executive Editor
Gem Rabanera, Project Editor
Alia Bales, Production Editor
Jess Estrella, Senior Graphic Designer
Trey Soto, Licensing Coordinator
Natalie Piccotti, Director of Marketing
Kassie Graves, Vice President of Editorial
Jamie Giganti, Director of Academic Publishing

3970 Sorrento Valley Blvd., Ste. 500, San Diego, CA 92121

Contents

Section IX   Collaboration and Partnerships   195

Preface

THIS TEXTBOOK HAS BEEN DESIGNED TO be used in college-level graduate courses in the area of special education. This text provides the learner with several different topic areas within the field of special education that are often times controversial in nature. Many of the scenarios provided within each chapter are examples of issues of which the authors have personally been a part. The goal of this book is to provide learners with information about concepts that they will likely need to think critically about at some point in their educational careers. Unfortunately there is not one solution to fix every situation. Most issues in education are extremely subjective in nature and the problems need to be looked at through many different lenses. It is the authors' hope that learners will begin to see differing sides and options in which problems may be solved.

Throughout our years within the special education department at Slippery Rock University, we were assigned to teach a graduate-level course titled "Contemporary Issues in Special Education." The course was designed for our graduate special education students with the premise of having the students think critically about common issues within the field of special education. The text being used was decent, but it was structured in a way that provided two differing sides to a problem. We found that our students often came up with differing opinions and ideas that were not addressed by the current textbook author. So, after many conversations on what we wanted from our graduate students, we decided to write our own text that gave readers general information about a given topic and also allowed learners to really express their own ideas, thoughts, and conclusions through thoughtful thinking and extension activities in each chapter.

We have had a relationship with Cognella Publishing for another textbook utilized in our undergraduate program, so we decided to partner with them again for this project.

We hope that this textbook is not only a win for our students but also for other instructors looking for a text like this one.

We sincerely hope that you will find the chapters in this text well written and organized to provide current and future educators the necessary tools and knowledge to make the best decisions possible that allow them to do their job, follow the required laws and regulations, and most importantly are in students' best interest.

Happy reading!

Acknowledgments

THIS TEXTBOOK WAS DEVELOPED FROM A variety of experiences and knowledge gained through the various teaching opportunities we have had throughout our time serving students with special needs. A huge thank you to the incredible colleagues, master's and doctoral students, and local administrators who have assisted in writing some of the chapters in this textbook. We truly appreciate your willingness to be a part of this endeavor and to share your expertise and experiences. Thank you also to the members of the Department of Special Education at Slippery Rock University for the opportunity to be part of a phenomenal group of educators.

Thank you for the support and guidance from all the staff at Cognella Publishing, especially John Remington and Gem Rabanera. You made this idea for a textbook a reality.

And last but not least, a big thank you to our spouses (Shawn and Craig) and to our children (Finn, Gemma, Polly, Jett, Gabe, Luke, and Sloan) for their support, love, and patience as we spent time away to work on this textbook.

Section I

Autism

Chapter 1

Applied Behavior Analysis
Should ABA be the Basis for Educating Students with Autism?

Christopher W. Tarr

PICTURE THIS: Have you ever visited a special education classroom and observed that each student is learning different, individualized skills via different and unique teaching strategies? Or maybe you witnessed a teacher reward a student each and every time he or she completed a simple task? Have you ever walked into a school restroom and observed pictures on the wall illustrating and describing each step of how to complete a bathroom routine? Have you ever wondered what type of student or students require such individualized attention that rewards every success or those who require a visual reminder of every step in a seemingly simple routine? Providing such individualized attention, providing constant rewards for desired behaviors, and directly teaching each step of a simple task is the responsibility of every teacher or clinician who works with individuals with autism.

What Is the Issue?

Statistics suggest that 13–20% of children in the United States experience a mental health disorder in a given year (Perou et al., 2013). Autism spectrum disorder is the fifth most prevalent childhood disorder, and it affects roughly 1.1% of all children aged 3–17 years old (Perou et al., 2013). Autism is considered one of the most frequent of the mental health disorders and one of the most debilitating (Matson & Lovullo, 2008). Autism was once thought to be a rare disorder, occurring 1 in every 2,500 births (Hallahan, Kauffman, & Pullen, 2015). Current data reveal that the prevalence rate for autism is 1 out of every 59 births (Centers for Disease Control and Prevention, 2018). It is suggested that autism is the fastest growing disability on the planet (Lawlis, 2010).

The term "autism" means to revert inward, isolate from others, or to live in a world of isolation (Shorter & Wachtel, 2013). Individuals who are diagnosed with autism display delays in communication and social skills and exhibit repetitive patterns of behavior. Children with autism are socially disconnected, isolated, and unable to socially interact due to their inability to effectively interact with the surrounding environment for various reasons. Most children with autism have difficulties taking in and processing sensory information. It is reported that 80–90% of children with autism have sensory processing difficulties (Schaaf & Miller, 2005). These sensory difficulties and the presence of stereotypic, repetitive behaviors make it difficult for these children to interact with their surroundings.

Autism is considered a neurodevelopmental disorder, which results from aberrant connections between areas of the brain. However, more recently, others would argue that autism is a systems disorder. Dr. Mark Hyman, a functional and integrative health medical doctor, believes that "autism is a systemic body disorder that affects the brain and body" (Hyman, 2018). Hyman (2018) further explains that a toxic environment triggers certain genes in individuals who are susceptible to autism.

All individuals diagnosed with autism experience deficits in communication, social skills, and the presence of repetitive and restricted patterns of behavior. However, each individual may experience the deficits in different ways and experience the deficits to varying degrees. Autism is considered a spectrum disorder with individuals diagnosed in severity from mild to severe. Individuals on the mild end of the autism spectrum may present with higher communication, social, and adaptability skills. While individuals on the more severe end of the autism spectrum may present with lower communication, lower social, and lower adaptability skills, persons diagnosed with an autism spectrum disorder are part of a very heterogeneous population.

In addition to the core symptoms, a high percentage of children with autism experience anxiety, hyperactivity, and problems with sensory integration, and they engage in problem behaviors. Problem behaviors have become a focus of research. Researchers are studying problem behaviors in an effort to identify efficient and effective interventions. These behaviors have the potential to harm and damage. Problem behaviors are defined as those behaviors that interfere with a person's ability to function (Minshawi et al., 2014). Such behaviors include physical aggression, verbal aggression, property destruction, tantrums, stereotypic behaviors and self-injurious behaviors (Minshawi et al., 2014). A research synthesis conducted by Horner, Carr, Strain, Todd, and Reed (2002) reported that the most frequently studied problem behaviors in individuals with autism are self-injury, aggression, and stereotypic behaviors. Epidemiological studies suggest that 13–30% of children with autism engage in problem behaviors that require intervention (Horner et al., 2002).

Problem behaviors create a barrier to integration (Elliott, Dobbin, Rose, & Soper, 1994). Horner, Carr, Strain, Todd, and Reed (2002) conducted a research synthesis on the interventions used to decrease problem behaviors. Horner and colleagues (2002) cited numerous studies that suggested that children with autism who engage in problem behaviors experience higher rates of exclusion in the educational, social, and communal settings. They stated that problem behaviors such as physical aggression, self-injury, and stereotypic behaviors are major barriers to proper educational and social development. They also stressed the importance of identifying effective interventions due to the belief that once a problem behavior becomes a part of a child's repertoire, the problem behavior will not decrease without intervention.

Irene (2015) reported that parents of children with autism experience more psychological stress, worry, emotional burnout, physical health issues, and social isolation than parents of children who are not diagnosed with autism. The increased emotional and physical distress is partly due to problematic behaviors. The chronicity and severity of autism also contributes the unstable emotional state of parents and siblings (Irene, 2015). Irene (2015) stated that the lack of language, the bizarre behaviors, and tantrums likely increase the anxiety experienced by parents of children with autism. Irene (2015) suggested that the deficits and behaviors are not the only source of stress for parents. Elevated anxiety levels in parents of children with autism are likely due to concern about the permanence of the diagnosis, the refusal of society to accept the child's behaviors, and the low levels of social support (Irene, 2015).

Like Irene (2015), Myers, Mackintosh, and Goin-Kochel (2009) also reported that problematic behaviors are a major source of stress for parents. Myers and colleagues (2009) stated that problematic behaviors are hard to manage and therefore cause chaos throughout the household. Problematic behaviors can leave parents feeling socially isolated and locked in their own homes. Many parents fear taking their children into the community due to the potential the child may cause a scene (Myers et al., 2009). Therefore, autism is considered among the most stressful of all the childhood developmental disabilities (Gray, 2006). Myers and colleagues (2009) report that longitudinal studies have suggested that problem behaviors are stable across years.

Each individual with autism has very specific, unique, and complex needs. It has often been said, "If you have seen one person with autism, then you have seen one person with autism." Every individual with autism presents with a unique set of needs and challenges. The diverse needs and challenges, coupled with the intrusive and invasive nature of the characteristics of autism, require many individuals with this diagnosis to seek out special support or specialized instruction in all domains of their lives. Individuals with autism often require a comprehensive and diverse team of specialized therapists. For instance, individuals with autism often require specialized instruction in the educational setting and specialized therapies within the home and community settings. Many individuals with autism participate in speech, occupational, developmental, and behavioral therapies within and outside of the formal educational setting.

Many different types of interventions and therapies have been successfully implemented with individuals with autism to decrease problem behaviors and increase appropriate behaviors. Many interventions are considered evidence-based practices (EBP). Some of these include discrete trial training, functional communication training, physical exercise, social narratives, and the Treatment and Education of Autistic and Communication related handicapped Children (TEACCH) method. Some specialized therapies are commonly used with individuals with autism. These include speech therapy, occupational therapy, music therapy, vision therapy, sensory integration therapy, and chelation.

Roughly 6 million students in the United States are identified as children who require special education services (Hallahan, Kauffman, & Pullen, 2015). An increasing number of these students are children diagnosed with autism spectrum disorder. Research has demonstrated that students with autism lack the necessary skills to engage in observational learning and/or learn vicariously by watching others (Taylor & DeQuinzio, 2012). Therefore, educators must modify lessons to teach students directly. Hallahan, Kaufmann, and Pullen (2015) write that educational programming for students with autism should include direct instruction, natural environment teaching, and a behavior management system. Most teachers have little to no experience with creating behavior management techniques. How can teachers effectively and efficiently manage the diverse, individualized, intrusive, and invasive characteristics of autism? What techniques should be used?

Siri and Lyons (2010) suggest that autism is the result of the "perfect storm" of factors, meaning that individuals with autism are genetically predisposed for autism, but environmental factors triggers its onset. Integrative and functional medicine doctors and practitioners argue that autism is the result of many systems gone awry. They believe that autism is a systemic body disorder that affects the body and the brain. These doctors cite that 95% of individuals with autism have gut and stomach problems. Therefore, their interventions are medically based. Some of these interventions may include proper nutrition, sleep, exercise, and stress management. Some advocate for treatment via essential vitamins and supplements, such as vitamins B12, B6, D and A, folate, omega 3 fatty acids, magnesium, and zinc. Other medical interventions used are psychotropic medications and chelation, which is the process of ridding the body of toxic metals.

What Is Applied Behavior Analysis?

However, one of the most commonly used and the most successful interventions used to increase appropriate skills and decrease inappropriate behaviors in individuals with autism is applied behavior analysis (ABA). Simply stated, ABA is a science committed to the understanding and improvement of human behavior (Cooper, Heron & Heward, 2007). More specific, ABA is a scientific approach for discovering environmental variables that reliably influence socially significant behavior and for developing a technology of behavior change that takes practical advantage of those discoveries (Cooper et al., 2007). Applied behavior analysis strives to make changes in behavior that are socially valid by analyzing the relationship between the environmental variables and behavior.

Applied behavior analysis formally emerged in 1968 with the unveiling of the *Journal of Applied Behavior Analysis* (*JABA*) and the publication of "Some Current Dimensions of

Applied Behavior Analysis," by Baer, Wolf, and Risley (Cooper et al., 2007). This paper continues to be referred to as the most comprehensive description of the ABA. Baer, Wolf, and Risely (1968) demanded that ABA be applied, behavioral, analytic, technological, conceptually systematic, effective, and capable of appropriately generalized outcomes (Cooper et al., 2007). Additionally, Heward (2005) suggested that ABA should be accountable, public, doable, empowering, and optimistic.

In its simplest form, ABA adheres to the stimulus-response-stimulus (S-R-S) changes, three-term contingency model, developed by B.F. Skinner. Skinner described this model as operant behavior. Skinner posed that operant behaviors are not the result of preceding stimuli, but are the result of stimulus changes that followed the behavior in the past (Cooper et al., 2007). In other words, behaviors are influenced by what rewards/punishments are presented following behaviors. Applied behavior analysis is a comprehensive discipline that follows the S-R-S model. Applied behavior analysis identifies and defines problem behaviors and measures change in behavior as a result of the presentation of rewards and/or punishments. Individuals who obtain a board-certified behavior analyst (BCBA) certification have extensive knowledge in ways to select, define, and measure behavior. They are also proficient in using proven techniques to evaluate and analyze behavior change, as well reinforcement and punishment techniques.

The techniques used by behavior analysts have demonstrated success in increasing socially desirable behaviors, decreasing socially unacceptable behaviors, and teaching new behaviors to individuals with autism. Applied behavior analysis is a preferred method of decreasing aberrant behavior in individuals with autism (Foxx, 2008). Some ABA techniques that have been used to decrease behaviors are extinction procedures, differential reinforcement schedules, and antecedent intervention procedures such as functional communication training and noncontingent reinforcement. Foxx (2008) elaborates further by stating that "the only interventions that have been shown to produce comprehensive, lasting results in autism have been based on the principles of ABA" (p.832).

Comprehensive ABA intervention has led to increases in intellectual functioning, language development, acquisition of daily living skills, and social functioning in individuals with autism (Virues-Ortega, 2010). Some ABA techniques that have been successfully used to produce such positive results are imitation training, shaping procedures, task analysis, and chaining techniques.

While ABA has shown the ability to increase appropriate behaviors and decrease inappropriate behaviors in individuals with autism, some argue with its effectiveness. The What Works Clearinghouse helps administrators, educators, and clinicians make good evidence-based decisions by providing a central source of research. Regarding ABA, the What Works Clearinghouse declares that ABA produces mixed results. After reviewing two studies that met their criteria, the What Works Clearinghouse stated that ABA had shown possible positive effects on cognitive development, yet no effects on communication or social, emotional, behavioral, and functional skills.

What Does the Law Say?

Behavioral interventions and educational services rendered to individuals with autism are required, by federal law, to be supported by scientific research. There are three levels of scientific support. The most basic level of scientific support is research based. Research-based practices are techniques that have been studied but without scientific rigor. Next are scientific-based practices that have been published and reviewed by peers and have been replicated to demonstrate cause and effect. Finally, the most rigorous of all three levels are EBP. Evidence-based practices are practices that have been quantitatively researched to demonstrate a cause-and-effect relationship (Odom, Collet-Klingenberger, Rogers, & Hatton, 2010).

Most individuals with autism necessitate a comprehensive team of educators and specialized therapists within the educational, home, and community settings. Pennsylvania is a unique state in which individuals with autism qualify for free, state-funded, behavioral support within the home, community, and educational settings, through Pennsylvania's Office of Mental Health and Substance Abuse Services (OMHSAS). Individuals with autism, who are enrolled in the medical assistance program within OMHSAS, are eligible for access to a variety of levels of care and treatment. Each county within the commonwealth is required to select a managed care organization (MCO) to oversee these levels of care. The levels of care may vary from county to county. They can range from highly restrictive inpatient hospital settings to least restrictive case management services. All behavioral supports that are provided via these state-funded programs are required to be evidence-based practices.

One of Pennsylvania's more common levels of care, sought out by parents, are behavioral health rehabilitation services (BHRS). Community-based BHRS was first used in Pennsylvania in 1989. This level of care includes a behavioral specialist consultant (BSC), a mobile therapist (MT), and therapeutic staff support (TSS). Behavioral health services rendered by a BSC, MT, and/or a TSS take place in the home, community, and educational settings.

Behavioral specialist consultants and mobile therapists are master's degree–level clinicians. Behavioral specialist consultants are clinicians whose main functions are to assess the needs of the individuals, develop the appropriate interventions, and create an effective treatment plan. Mobile therapists render individual therapy sessions. Therapeutic staff support (TSS) are bachelor's degree–level clinicians who are responsible for implementing the behavioral strategies created by the BSC. All interventions used are required to be evidence-based practices (EBP).

In 2008, the Autism Insurance Act (Act 62) was passed and signed into law. Act 62 requires commercial insurance companies to cover treatment for individuals with autism. Because commercial insurance companies require that services be rendered by licensed clinicians, Pennsylvania created a behavior specialist license (BSL) through the State Board of Medicine. Of the many requirements for this license is completing 90 hours of training, of which 45 hours is on ABA. Additionally, in Pennsylvania all TSS who wish to work with individuals with autism are required to complete 6 hours of trainings specifically for the principles and practices of ABA. Pennsylvania's OMHSAS recognizes ABA as the "gold standard" of EBP for individuals with autism.

The EBP movement is observed in the educational system. On November 19, 1975 Congress established the Education Law for All Handicapped Children Act of 1975. The purpose of this act was to ensure that individuals with disabilities had access to an education and due process of law (Wright & Wright, 2012). The Act of 1975 has been amended and renamed numerous times. The most significant change occurred in 2004 when Congress authorized the Individuals with Disabilities Education Improvement Act (IDEA). The scope of this act expanded to include accountability and improved outcomes by emphasizing reading, early intervention, and research-based instruction by requiring that special education teachers be highly qualified (Wright & Wright, 2012). While ABA is not mandated by the IDEA, many parents, teachers, and administrators believe that techniques that adhere to the principles of ABA provide the best results.

How Does This Affect Schools?

The evidence-based movement in education and home and community support requires educators and therapists to identify and use only research-based techniques. However, one of the biggest barriers is getting research-proven techniques into practice. Administrators and clinicians are required to learn about the most effective interventions and hire qualified educators and therapists who can adequately implement the interventions. Administrators are challenged with finding resources to help them determine EBPs, time to train new and proven techniques, and changing staff philosophies (Odom & Hume, 2017). Administrators must decide whether they want to implement comprehensive treatment models, focused intervention practices, or a combination of both approaches. Comprehensive treatment models include the Denver Model, Learning Experiences and Alternate Program (LEAP), TEACCH, Princeton Child Development Institute, the May Institute, and the Lovaas Institute, which is heavily based on the principles of ABA.

In 2007, the Office of Special Education Programs within the United States Department of Education created and funded the National Professional Development Center on Autism Spectrum Disorders (NPDC). The NPDC was created to promote the use of EBP in programs for individuals of all ages with autism. One of the first responsibilities of the NPDC was to identify evidence-based practices.

The NPDC searched the literature for focus intervention practices only to identify EBP. Focused intervention practices are defined as strategies that educators and therapists use to teach specific skills to individuals with autism (Odom, Collet-Klingenberg, Rogers, & Hatton, 2010). The work of the NPDC resulted in the identification of 24 evidence-based practices. Many of the focused intervention practices identified as EBPs are based on the principles of ABA. For example, prompting, reinforcement, task analysis, chaining, discrete trial training, differential reinforcement schedules, extinction, parent-implemented interventions, peer-mediated interventions, and functional behavior assessment (FBA) were determined to be EBPs.

Additionally, the National Standards Project was developed by the National Autism Center to help educators, families, and clinicians navigate which interventions are deemed evidence based. In 2009 the National Standard Project revealed their results for EBPs for individuals with autism. The National Standards Project revealed 11 "established" treatments, 22 "emerging" treatments, and 5 "unestablished" treatments. The vast majority of the "established" treatments were based on behavioral research, including ABA (National Autism Center, 2018).

School administrators and organization leaders should also have knowledge of assessments that have been developed to determine an intervention as evidence based. For instance, the evaluative method, designed by Reichow, Volkmar, and Cicchetti (2008), was created to assess the rigor of studies that involved individuals with autism and to assist in determining if interventions were to be deemed evidence based. The evaluative method includes three instruments for both single-subject and group research designs. These instruments are the rubrics for the evaluation of research rigor, guidelines for the evaluation of research report strength, and criteria for determining of EBP. Reichow, Volkmar, and Cicchetti (2008) tested the reliability of the rubrics via field tests and communication interventions. Each of these tests revealed high agreement across applications and across individuals. Reichow, Volkmar, and Cicchetti (2008) stated that "the high agreement across applications and individuals support the evaluative method as a tool for reliably reviewing autism intervention research" (p. 1315). The validity of the evaluative method was assessed for concurrent validity, content validity, and face validity. The evaluative method was determined to have good to excellent validity.

What Is the Impact of Students Needing Special Education or 504 Plan Services?

The principles of ABA have had a tremendous impact on individuals with autism, students requiring special education, and students requiring a 504 plan. Educators use the principles of ABA on a daily basis. Teachers observe, define, and measure students' behaviors. They collect data on behaviors to establish individualized education plan (IEP) goals and objectives. Teachers break tasks down into smaller parts to help students learn. Finally, teachers implement reinforcement techniques to increase the occurrence of desired behaviors.

One of the most influential contributions from the principles of ABA was the development of the Functional Behavior Assessment and the functional analysis (FA). An FBA is a common practice used to decrease problem behaviors, specifically self-injurious behaviors. Functional behavior assessment is a broad term to describe a variation of procedures that aim to uncover the functions of behavior. The popularity of the FBA grew in 1997 when the federal government reauthorized IDEA. This reauthorization required the use of procedures similar to FAs.

The practice of FBA originated in the educational setting. Due to the IDEA, an increasing number of students with intellectual disabilities and autism were being educated in typical school settings. These children often exhibit problem behaviors, and some do not have the ability to communicate why they are demonstrating those behaviors. The FBA allows educators and school staff to observe and problem solve what is triggering and maintaining the problem behaviors.

FBA can be performed three different ways: direct method, indirect method, and FA, also termed experimental method. The direct method involves direct observations in natural settings. The indirect method involves interviews, rating scales, and checklists. The FA method entails the systematic manipulation of variables. A recent study among educators suggests that teachers perceive the FBA process as essential for developing effective interventions (Oliver, Pratt, & Normand, 2015). Oliver, Pratt, and Normand (2015) also report that the majority of teachers prefer the direct method over the experimental (FA) and indirect methods.

The FA method has a long history of decreasing self-injurious behaviors in people with autism. FA is the experimental process of determining the functions of behavior. Once the functions of behavior are determined, positive environmental manipulations are made to decrease the likelihood of self-injury behavior responses. Reviews of FA methodology have suggested that FAs result in determination of behavioral function in 94% of the cases in which they were applied (Dixon, Vogel, and Tarbox, 2012; Iwata et al., 1994). Understanding the functions of behavior when planning treatment is widely accepted as a best-practice standard (Dixon, Vogel, and Tarbox, 2012).

The marquee study that developed the FA protocol was conducted by Iwata, Dorsey, Slifer, Bauman, and Richman (1994). Iwata, Dorsey, and colleagues (1994) were the first to complete a comprehensive analysis of the environmental factors that increase the likelihood of aberrant behaviors. The work of Iwata, Dorsey, and colleagues (1994) showed that levels of aberrant behaviors vary across individuals and were increased under conditions of higher control. The majority of aberrant behaviors were the result of children wanting to escape demands, followed by wanting to gain attention or tangible objects, and automatic reinforcement (Iwata, Dorsey, et al., 1994).

In 2008, Pennsylvania created the Bureau of Autism Services (BAS) to oversee all services rendered to the individuals with autism in home, community, and educational settings. Because of the high success rate of FBAs to accurately identify functions of problem behaviors, which leads to the efficient identification of behavioral intervention, the BAS began requiring BSCs to offer FBAs to all individuals with autism beginning in 2009. The completion of FBAs is viewed as having significant value and is considered a "best practice" in home, community, and educational settings in Pennsylvania.

What Is the Impact on Students in General Education?

According to the *Diagnostic and Statistical Manual of Mental Health Disorders*, fifth edition, individuals with autism range in severity from "requiring very substantial support" to "requiring substantial support" to "requiring support" (American Psychiatric Association, 2013, p. 52). The severity level and the services available in each school district often determines an individual's educational placement. Some individuals with autism, who require very substantial support, cannot be adequately managed in home and educational settings. These individuals may require removal from the home and a transition to a residential treatment facility (RTF). These individuals are educated in the RTFs in a highly restrictive environment. Some students with autism require highly specialized autism schools. Others are educated in autism support classrooms within community school districts. An increasing number of students with autism are being educated in the mainstream classroom alongside their neurotypical peers. The increase in students with autism being educated alongside their peers provides opportunities for teachers and students to implement the principles of ABA with students with autism.

Many often associate ABA with a very intensive, time-consuming, and specialized type of treatment. Although ABA can be just that, it does not always require such high levels of expertise. In its most general form, anyone who rewards students for appropriate behaviors or punishes negative behaviors is applying the principles of ABA. Therefore, almost anyone can apply these principles to improve desired behaviors and decrease negative behaviors, even peers.

The delays in social skills experienced by individuals with autism create a barrier to social inclusion with neurotypical peers. Therefore, some schools engage in peer-mediated instruction and intervention activities. Some of these activities include lunch bunch groups, buddy systems, and peer tutoring. Peer-mediated support strategies involve peers providing support to their classmates with autism and are used to provide social learning opportunities through peer interaction, peer modeling, and peer reinforcement.

The basic components of peer-mediated strategies are based on ABA. A tremendous benefit of ABA interventions is that research has shown that parents and peers can successfully implement these strategies with success. Heitzman-Powell, Buzhardt, Rusinko, and Miller (2013) demonstrated that parents are able to learn and implement ABA interventions with success. In addition, peers have shown positive results when implementing intervention strategies (Bass & Mulick, 2007). Peer-mediated strategies have been shown to effectively teach students with autism a range of skills and behaviors including academic engagement, responding to others, understanding others, interacting with others in larger groups, and reciprocity. In addition, peer-mediated strategies also benefit students without disabilities academically and socially, as these students learn to appreciate diversity among students.

Conclusion

The prevalence for individuals to be diagnosed with autism spectrum disorder continues to be on the rise. Students with autism are becoming a larger proportion of our communities and educational settings. The IDEA requires that students with special needs receive educational practices that are based on research. Evidence-based practices are considered the most effective strategies and/or interventions. One of the more effective strategies to teach individuals with autism is ABA, which has been shown to be effective when administered in home and educational settings (Grindle, Kovshoff, Hastings, and Remington, 2009). Despite not being mandated by the IDEA, many believe that individuals with autism should be educated using strategies and/or interventions based on the principles of ABA.

References

American Psychiatric Association. (2013). *Diagnostic and statistical manual of mental disorders* (5th ed.). Washington, DC: Author.

Baer, D. M., Wolf, M. M., & Risely, T. R. (1968). Some current dimensions on applied behavior analysis. *Journal of Applied Behavior Analysis, 1*(1), 91–97.

Bass, J. D., & Mulick, J. A. (2007). Social play skill enhancement of children with autism using peers and siblings as therapists. *Psychology in Schools, 44*(7), 727–735. doi:10.1002/pits.20261

Centers for Disease Control and Prevention. (2018). *Autism prevalence slightly higher in CDC's ADDM network*. Retrieved from https://www.cdc.gov/media/releases/2018/p0426-autism-prevalence.html

Cooper, J. O., Heron, T. E., & Heward, W. L. (2007). *Applied behavior analysis* (2nd ed.). Upper Saddle River, NJ: Pearson.

Dixon, D. R., Vogel, T., & Tarbox, J. (2012). A brief history of functional analysis and applied behavior analysis. In J. L. Matson (Ed.), *Functional assessment for challenging behaviors* (pp. 3–24). Retrieved from http://link.springer.com/chapter/10.1007%2F978-1-4614-3037-7_2#page-1

Elliott, R. O., Dobbin, A. R., Rose, G. D., & Soper, H.V. (1994). Vigorous, aerobic exercise versus general motor training activities: Effects on maladaptive and stereotypic behaviors of adults with both autism and mental retardation. *Journal of Autism and Developmental Disorders*, 24(5), 565–576.

Foxx, R. M. (2008). Applied behavior analysis treatment of autism: The state of the art. *Child and Adolescent Psychiatric Clinics of North America*, 17(4), 821–834.

Gray, D. E. (2006). Coping over time: the parents of children with autism. *Journal of Disability Research*, 50(12), 970–976.

Grindle, C. F., Kovshoff, H., Hastings, R. P., & Remington, B. (2009). Parents' experiences of home-based applied behavior analysis programs for young children with autism. *Journal of Autism and Developmental Disorders*, 39(1), 42–56. doi:10.1007/s10803-008-0597-z

Hallahan, D., Kauffman, J. K., & Pullen, P. C. (2015). *Exceptional learners: An introduction to special education*. Boston, MA: Pearson.

Heitzman-Powell, L. S., Buzhardt, J., Rusinko, L. C., & Miller, T. M. (2013). Formative evaluation of an ABA outreach training program for parents of children with autism in remote areas. *Focus on Autism and Other Developmental Disabilities*, 29(1), 23–38. doi:10.1177/1088357613504992

Heward, W. L. (2005). Reasons applied behavior analysis is good for education and why those reasons have been insufficient. In W. L. Heward, T. E. Heron, N. A. Neef, S. M. Peterson, D. M. Sainato, G. Cartledge, R. Gardner, III, L. D. Peterson, S. B Hersh, & J. C. Dardig (Eds.), *Focus on behavior analysis in education: Achievements, challenges, and opportunities* (pp. 316–348). Upper Saddle River, NJ: Merrill/Prentice Hall.

Horner, R. H., Carr, E. G., Strain, P. S., Todd, A. W., & Reed, H. K. (2002). Problem behavior interventions for young children with autism: A research synthesis. *Journal of Autism and Developmental Disorders*, 32(5), 423–446.

Hyman, M. (2018). *Broken brain docuseries: Episode 4 ADHD and autism*. Retrieved from https://www.youtube.com/watch?v=H4NsEUj4--E

Irene, D. (2015). The experiences of parents for emotional interaction with children with autism: A systematic approach. *Journal of Psychiatry*, 18(5). doi:10.4172/2378-5756.1000310

Iwata, B., Pace, G. M., Dorsey, M. F., Zarcone, J. R., Vollmer, T. R., Smith, R. G., ... & Rodgers, T. A. (1994). The functions of self-injurious behavior: An experimental-epidemiological analysis. *Journal of Applied Behavior Analysis*, 27(2), 215–240.

Iwata, B. A., Dorsey, M. F., Slifer, K. J., Bauman, K. E., & Richman, G. S. (1994). Toward a functional analysis of self-injury. *Journal of Applied Behavior Analysis*, 27(2), 197–209.

Lawlis, F. (2010). The autism answer: Finding the compass through the current of chaos and destructive paths. Middleton, DE: Youthapedia.

Lee, S., Odom, S. L., & Loftin, R. (2007). Social engagement with peers and stereotypic behavior of children with autism. *Journal of Positive Behavior Interventions*, 9(2), 67–79.

Lovaas, I., Litrownik, A., & Mann, R. (1971). Response latencies to auditory stimuli in autistic children engaged in self-stimulatory behavior. *Behavior Research and Therapy*, 9(1), 39–49.

Lovaas, I., Newsom, C., & Hickman, C. (1987). Self-stimulatory behavior and perceptual reinforcement. *Journal of Applied Behavior Analysis*, 20(1), 45–68.

Matson, J. L., & LoVullo, S. V. (2008). A review of behavioral treatments for self-injurious behaviors of persons with autism spectrum disorders. *Behavior Modification*, 32(1), 61–76.

Militerni, R., Bravaccio, C., Falco, C., Fico, C., & Palermo, M. T. (2002). Repetitive behaviors in autistic disorder. *European Child & Adolescent Psychiatry*, 11(5), 210–218.

Minshawi, N. H., Hurwitz, S., Fodstad, J. C., Biebl, S., Morriss, D. H., and McDougle, C. J. (2014). The association between self-injurious behaviors and autism spectrum disorders. *Psychology Research and Behavior Management*, 7, 125–136.

Morrison, K., & Rosales-Ruiz, J. (1997). The effect of object preferences on task performance and stereotypy in a child with autism. *Research in Developmental Disabilities*, 18(2), 127–137.

Myers, B. J., Mackintosh, V. H., & Goin-Kochel, R. P. (2009). "My greatest joy and my greatest heart ache": Parents' own words on how having a child in the autism spectrum has affected their lives and their families' lives. *Research in Autism Spectrum Disorders*, 3(3), 670–684.

National Autism Center. (2018). Significant findings. Retrieved from https://www.nationalautismcenter.org/national-standards-project/.../significant-findings...

Odom, S. L, Collet-Klingenberg, L., Rogers, S. J., & Hatton, D. D. (2010). Evidence-based practices in interventions for children and youth with autism spectrum disorders. In M. Byrnes (Ed.), *Taking sides: Clashing views in special education* (6th ed.) (pp. 416–441). New York, NY: McGraw Hill.

Odom, S. L., & Hume, K. A. (2017, November 28). *Use of evidence-bases practices*. Retrieved from https://glenwood.org/wp-content/uploads/2013/06/article-evidence-based-practices-in-interventions-for-children-and-youth-with-ASDs.pdf

Oliver, A. C., Pratt, L. A., & Normand, M. P. (2015). A survey of functional behavior assessment methods used by behavior analysts in practice. *Journal of Applied Behavior Analysis*, 48(4), 817–829.

Perou, R., Bitsko, R. H., Blumberg, S. J., Pastor, P., Ghandour, R., Gfroerer, J. C., ... & Huang, L. N. (2013, May 17). *Preview*. Retrieved from http://www.cdc.gov/mmwr/preview/mmwrhtml/su6202a1.htm?s_cid =su6202a1_w

Reichow, B., Volkmar, F. R., & Cicchetti, D. V. (2008). Development of the evaluative method for evaluating and determining evidence-based practices in autism. *Journal of Autism and Developmental Disorders*, 38(7), 1311–1319.

Runco, M. A., Charlop, M. H., & Schreibman, L. (1986). The occurrence of autistic children's self-stimulation as a function of familiar versus unfamiliar stimulus conditions. *Journal of Autism and Developmental Disorder*, 16(1), 31–44.

Schaaf, R. C., & Miller, L. J. (2005). Occupational therapy using a sensory integrative approach for children with developmental disabilities. *Mental Retardation and Developmental Disabilities Research Reviews*, 11(2), 143–148.

Shorter, E., & Wachtel, L. E. (2013). Childhood catatonia, autism, and psychosis past and present: Is there an "iron triangle?" *Acta Psychiatrica Scandinavica*, 128(1), 21–33. doi.org/10.1111/acps.12082

Siri, K., & Lyons, T. (2010). Cutting edge therapies for autism 2010–2011. In M. Byrnes (Ed.), *Taking sides: Clashing views in special education* (6th ed.) (pp. 416-441). New York, NY: McGraw Hill.

Taylor, B. A., & DeQuinzio, J. A. (2012). Observational learning and children with autism. *Behavior Modification*, 36(3), 341–360. doi:10.1177/0145445512443981

Virues-Ortega, J. (2010). Applied behavior analytic intervention for autism in early childhood: Meta-analysis, meta-regression, and dose response meta-analysis of multiple outcomes. *Clinical Psychology Review*, 30(4), 387–399.

Wright, P. W. D., & Wright, P. D. (2012). History of special education law. In P. W. D. Wright & P. D. Wright (Eds.), *Special education law* (2nd ed.) (pp. 11–16). Hartfield, VA: Harbor House Law Press.

EXTENSION ACTIVITIES

Discussion Questions

1. Think of the type of teaching strategies and/or interventions that you are currently using with your students. Are the strategies and/or interventions research based, scientific based, or evidence based? How do you know?

2. One of the bigger barriers schools and/or organizations face with the implementation of evidence-based practices is the lack of transition of strategies and/or interventions from research to practice. Imagine you are a school administrator. What process do you utilize to educate your staff on current research and how to implement such strategies and/or interventions in the school setting?

3. Do you currently use strategies and/or interventions that are based on the principles of ABA? If so, what training have you received to adequately implement these strategies and/or interventions? Why do you choose to use such strategies?

4. If you are not currently using strategies and/or interventions based on the principles of ABA, which strategies and/or interventions could you use? What training have you received to adequately implement these strategies and/or interventions? Why have you chosen these strategies and/or interventions?

Discussion Paper

After reading this chapter, find a minimum of two additional articles that support this topic and write a double-spaced discussion paper following APA guidelines, including a bibliography page, to address the following in your paper:

- Before reading this chapter, my opinion on this issue was _____.

- In your own words, what is the issue at hand?

- Analyze what you see as the two sides of this issue.

- Identify a perceived misconception from either side. (When doing this, list the actual sentence(s) or portion of the sentence citing the page number that you are making reference to, then write your response as to why you think it is a misconception. The key word is "perceived.")

- And finally, which side do you personally agree with more and why? (Refer to your personal experiences, here. If you have dealt with this issue in your personal life, work, teaching, etc., include that information in your answer.)

- Make sure to include in-text citations (when appropriate) from the supporting articles that you found.

Chapter 2

Sensory Processing Disorders and Sensory Friendly Classrooms
Can They Become the Norm?

Jessica L. Patton

PICTURE THIS: You are a brand new teacher at a school district that fosters the inclusive classroom. Tonight is the district's Meet the Teacher night. As you welcome your new students and their families, some families are drawn to a specific space in your room. In this space you have an exercise ball, a beanbag chair, room-darkening curtains, a bubble lamp, plush carpet, and plastic bins of rice. You overhear the families talking amongst themselves about the space, asking why it is here and if it is appropriate for their child's classroom. How do you address the families and their questions regarding the space?

What Is the Issue?

People continuously gather information from their environment to perform daily activities through the use of eight sensory systems. The most commonly known systems are visual (sight), auditory (hearing), tactile (touch), olfactory (smell), and gustatory (taste). People also utilize two less commonly known senses—vestibular, the sense of knowing where our body is in space, and proprioceptive, the sense of balance. The least known sensory system is the interoceptive system, which detects the responses that guide regulation in hunger, heart rate, respiration, and elimination (Miller, 2014). Sensory processing is the way the nervous system receives input from our senses and interprets the input into responses. Most individuals naturally engage in conscious or subconscious acts that meet their specific sensory needs. Have you ever caught yourself tapping your pen while completing a challenging test? Do you pace the floor while you're talking on the phone? Have you ever found yourself bouncing your leg up and down while waiting for your turn at the doctor's office? These are all sensory strategies we naturally do to regulate our sensory needs. Our bodies and minds seem to automatically know what sensory input allows us to function appropriately within our environment.

When an individual's senses do not accurately relay information from the environment to his or her brain, abnormal responses may result. This "traffic jam" that prohibits specific parts of the brain from receiving information required to interpret sensory information was once referred to as sensory integration dysfunction but is now referred to as sensory processing disorder (SPD) (Miller, 2014). There are three types of SPD: (a) sensory over-responsivity, which is associated with hyperactivity; (b) sensory under-responsivity, which is often mislabeled as laziness; and (c) sensory seeking, which is often mislabeled as impulsivity and clumsiness (Levi-Shackleford, 2015).

SPD is not recognized in the *Diagnostic and Statistical Manual of Mental Disorders,* fifth edition (DSM-5) (American Psychological Association (APA), 2013) as a stand-alone disorder. Experts agree that some children demonstrate unusual and sometimes problematic sensory responses. However, they disagree whether there is sufficient scientific evidence to support SPD as an independent disorder listed in the DSM-5 (Arky, 2017). The current research demonstrates that children who experience sensory processing issues early in life could be later diagnosed with attention deficit/hyperactivity disorder (ADHD), anxiety, and/or most commonly, autism spectrum disorder (ASD) (Arky, 2017; Levi-Shackleford, 2015). According the DSM-5 (APA, 2013), specific sensory processing symptoms are not listed under the diagnostic criteria for anxiety. Regarding the diagnosis of ADHD, symptoms include "hyperactivity-impulsivity that interferes with functioning or development," but specific descriptions of the sensory processing symptoms are not included (APA, 2013, p. 59. However, the DSM-5 (2013) specifically includes sensory processing symptoms as the "hyper- or hypo-reactivity to sensory input or unusual interest in sensory aspects of the environment" as diagnostic criteria for ASD (APA, 2013, p. 50). Within the diagnostic criteria, examples are provided such as (a) the obvious indifference to pain and temperature, (b) specific sounds or textures that cause aversive responses, (c) excessive touching or smelling of objects, and (d) the visual fascination with movement or lights.

Despite the debate regarding the inclusion of SPD as an official diagnosis in the DSM-5 (APA, 2013), experts recognize the need for sensory processing identification and treatment due to the increase in affected populations. Research by Miller (2014) indicates that SPD affects at least 1 in 20 individuals in the general population. Her research has also found that the prevalence of SPD in individuals who are gifted, diagnosed with ADHD, ASD, and fragile X syndrome is much higher. The Center for Disease Control and Prevention's (CDC) (2016) National Survey of Children's Health reports approximately 9.4% (6.1 million) of children 2 to 17 years of years of age have been diagnosed with ADHD. Additionally, the CDC's (2018) Autism and Developmental Disabilities Monitoring (ADDM) Network reports approximately one in 59 children aged 8 years are diagnosed with ASD. These statistics only consider the children who have received an official diagnosis. Research conducted by the

Sensory Processing Disorder Scientific Work Group suggest that one in six children have sensory symptoms that are severe enough to impact their ability to perform daily functions (Ben-Sasson, Carter, & Briggs Gowan, 2009). Considering the increase in prevalence rates in all affected populations and the suggested number of undiagnosed cases, there is a high probability teachers will be expected to educate students with sensory processing challenges in their classrooms.

What Does the Law Say?

Under the federal law Individuals with Disabilities Education Act (IDEA), students who have a disability or who are thought to have a disability are entitled to a nondiscriminatory evaluation to determine the need for special education. For a student to qualify for special education, he or she must have a diagnosed disability under one of IDEA's disability categories, and his or her disability must adversely impact his or her education. Pennsylvania's special education regulations mandated by the IDEA are housed within what are referred to as Chapter 14 regulations. Each state is obligated to have its own version of the IDEA. It can make regulations within that state more stringent but cannot lower its standards below what IDEA mandates.

The determination of eligibility is made on an individual basis by the multidisciplinary team based on the results of an evaluation. The evaluation process is started after parental permission is obtained and must be concluded within 60 days from the receipt of parental consent to produce an evaluation report (ER). The ER contains information regarding a student's performance on a variety of assessment tools that gather functional, developmental, and academic information. Other information included in an ER is a review of student records, his or her present levels of performance, parental input, observations, and other assessment data provided by therapists and experts.

Once a student is found eligible for special education, the evaluation team will develop an individualized education program (IEP). The IEP is developed annually by the IEP team, which minimally includes the parents, special education teacher, regular education teacher, and local education agency (LEA) representative. Based on the student's evaluation, the IEP team develops IEP components including (a) present levels of academic achievement and functional performance, (b) measurable annual goals, (c) how the student's progress will be measured, (d) special education and related services, (e) supplementary aids and services, (f) an explanation of the extent the student will not participate with nondisabled students in the regular classroom and other activities, (g) projected starting and ending dates, (f) and transition planning when age appropriate. An IEP directs every aspect of the student special education program. A key component found within the law is that related services must be provided in conformity with the child's IEP. IDEA requires states to enact polices that ensure all students with disabilities are provided a free appropriate public education (FAPE). The right to FAPE entitles students with disabilities the right to special education and related services. Special education is "specially designed instruction at no charge to the parents or guardians, to meet the unique needs of a child with a disability" (IDEA, 20 U.S.C. § 1404[a][16]). This means that public schools are required to provide special education and related services to eligible students at no cost.

SPD does not, in and of itself, meet the criteria for a qualifying disability category under Chapter 14. However, students who have sensory processing disorder as a comorbid diagnosis with a recognized disability category, such as autism, can receive special education and related services to address their sensory needs. If a student experiences sensory processing concerns but does not have a comorbid diagnosis that qualifies under Chapter 14, he or she may be eligible for a Section 504 plan. Section 504 of the Rehabilitation Act of 1973 was enacted to protect individuals with disabilities and significant impairments from discrimination. It focuses on putting in place accommodations, modifications, services, and improved building accessibility for all students to have equal access to education. Students who have a physical or mental impairment that substantially limits at least one major life activity but are not in need of special education services may qualify for protections under Section 504. Some examples of major life activities include walking, seeing, hearing, speaking, breathing, reading, writing, completing math calculations, working, self-care, and completing manual tasks. Under this definition, students who experience significant impairment due to sensory processing challenges could qualify for reasonable accommodations and modifications to ensure they have equal access to the education provided to students without disabilities or significant impairments. To determine a student's eligibility, the school must perform an evaluation that accumulates information from a variety of sources prior to developing a Section 504 plan. This plan does not require public schools to provide an individualized education program nor does it provide the same protections that are available to students with an IEP under IDEA.

How Does This Affect Schools?

Students with SPD and undiagnosed sensory processing challenges may experience internal and external sensations much differently than their typically developing peers. These sensations and their brain's inability to interpret these sensations can affect the student's ability to learn in the classroom. Teachers have reported common disturbances related to sensory processing challenges. Gross motor issues are observed as balance problems, clumsy walking, poor hand and eye coordination, and frequent tripping. Students with SPD may present with messy handwriting as well as coloring and cutting outside of the lines.

Some students may experience interactions with the environment that results in distraction and problem behaviors. Teachers report some students with sensory processing challenges lack energy and have poor arousal. Other students may lack organization, have poor future planning skills, and have difficulty with social interaction, impulsivity, and attention span. Teachers have also reported students with sensory processing challenges may have poor test-taking skills due to distractions such as noises from the heater or air conditioning, hallway noise, movement, and smells.

Some students with sensory processing challenges experience tactile hypersensitivity to smell, taste, and textures. A student may want to wear sunglasses in class to avoid the bright florescent lighting, which is commonly used in school buildings. Other students may cover their ears during fire drills or avoid places with loud noises such as a gymnasium when basketballs are bouncing on the wood floor. Some students may avoid the gymnasium locker room, people wearing perfume, or areas that have just been cleaned to avoid strong smells. Students with tactile hypersensitivity may avoid participating during art class or completing craft projects that are messy and sticky. Some students with sensory processing challenges do not like being touched or being in close proximity to others. Teachers have observed students with SPD to wear specific or the same clothing and shoes to avoid tags, certain textures, or tightness. Some students will not buy school lunch and prefer to bring their own due to their sensitivity to spicy, tart, or the texture of foods. Teachers may observe students with SPD to seek swinging or spinning during recess for vestibular input.

Sensory friendly learning environments help students with SPD and sensory processing challenges by promoting calming and/or stimulation on an individual basis. This type of environment also provides more opportunities for learning by increasing the student's arousal and attention. Other positive impacts for students who can regulate their sensory needs in their classroom are better direction following, more time on tasks, a decrease in negative behavior, and more motivation to use the sensory area to self-regulate. Sensory friendly learning environments are credited with improving the student's mood and providing relaxation for all students as well, especially those with depression and anxiety-related conditions. Such environments can also help students with vision difficulties, language difficulties, learning disabilities, and emotional disturbances.

Sensory friendly environments not only help students with sensory challenges to feel more comfortable and give them the ability to regulate their sensory needs in their own classroom, they also keep them in their least restrictive environment (LRE). Federal law requires school districts to provide equitable services for students with disabilities. If schools do not provide such services, they must send students outside of the district to receive such services. By sending students outside of their home district for services, students and their families may feel less connected to their community. If schools do not provide equitable services, whether they are within their district or outside of their district, they may face litigation. Families of children with disabilities could send their children to private school and take the district to court to pay the cost of tuition. The child's home district is also responsible for the child's transportation to and from the private school at an additional cost. Setting up a sensory area in the student's classroom keeps students within their own communities and is more cost effective for school districts.

To create a sensory friendly classroom, the modifications to typical classrooms can be affordable and easily maintained. Ultimately, the space, materials, equipment, and their uses are determined by the student's IEP or 504 plan. Since the space can be used by other students, the classroom teacher can add additional materials to promote the universal effect. There are several inexpensive materials that are commonly used in a classroom sensory area. A mirror provides students visual feedback and promotes body awareness. Visual and audio input can also come from a bubble tube, which may have different colored lights and ocean sounds. Visual overstimulation can be reduced by soft or dimmed lighting by using a lower-watt bulb in a small lamp or by using a darker lamp shade. Overhead fluorescent lighting can be dimmed with dark pieces of cloth. To reduce audio stimulation, the sensory area may have a small sound machine or noise-canceling headphones. A small white board may provide an area for fine motor activities or a way to communicate by writing or drawing feelings or needs. A Lego wall could be used for fine motor, organizing, or calming activities. Tactile bins are plastic storage containers filled with beans, rice, and sand that provide a low-demand activity with high sensory input. Students can use their hands to draw, write, or find objects in the bins for a calming effect. A weighted blanket provides deep pressure, which can be very calming for some students. Beanbag chairs and a soft blanket provide comfort and relaxation. To address proprioception needs and to provide full body input, an occupational therapist may recommend a heavy work activity such as bouncing on an exercise ball or jumping on a small exercise trampoline. These two pieces of equipment require a larger space and must be carefully considered.

What Is the Impact on Students Needing Special Education or 504 Plan Services?

When a student experiences sensory challenges that adversely impact his or her educational success and has an IEP, an occupational therapist is added to the IEP team through the evaluation process. Once the evaluation is complete and the student's eligibility for additional special education services is determined, the IEP will add occupational therapy to the student's IEP under related services. Related services are any developmental, corrective, or supportive services that students need to benefit from special education (Wright & Wright, 2017).

If the student is not eligible for an IEP, the use of sensory equipment can be written in the student's Section 504 plan.

IDEA states that special education services and related services, such as occupational therapy, must be provided to the students in their LRE. LRE ensures students with disabilities are educated with their nondisabled peers to the maximum extent possible. There is a continuum of least restrictive environments ranging from consultation and accommodations in the student's general education classroom to the most restrictive setting such as pull-out therapy sessions. Pull-out occupational sessions require the student to be removed from the general education setting.

Most students with disabilities who have sensory processing challenges use equipment to assist with their sensory regulation in their general education classroom. Sensory equipment is recommended by the IEP team, usually based on the expertise of the occupational therapist, and is listed in the student's IEP under the specially designed instruction section. Sensory equipment and its use falls under the definition of supplementary aids and services. This means aids, services, and supports that are provided in regular education classes that enable students with disabilities to be educated with their nondisabled peers to the maximum extent possible (Wright & Wright, 2017).

According to IDEA, sensory equipment also falls under the definition of assistive technology devices and services. Public schools are mandated by IDEA to provide assistive technology devices and services, or both, to a student with a disability if such devices and services are required as part of the student's special education, related services, or supplementary aids and services (Wright & Wright, 2017). The term "assistive technology device" is defined as any item, piece of equipment, or product system, whether acquired commercially off the shelf, modified, or customized, that is used to increase, maintain, or improve functional capabilities of a child with a disability (Wright & Wright, 2017). Most people only think of assistive technology as a "talker," which is a communication app loaded onto a tablet to assist students with communication needs. They do not think an exercise ball, mini trampoline, or a beanbag chair are considered technology. However, according the IDEA's definition, these low-tech items are considered assistive technology as long as the student demonstrates educational benefit with their use. To properly use sensory equipment, students with sensory needs also benefit from assistive technology services. The term "assistive technology service" is defined as any service that directly assists a child with a disability in the selection, acquisition, or use of an assistive technology device (Wright & Wright, 2017). This definition also includes the evaluation of the student's needs including selecting, fitting, customizing, adapting, maintaining, repairing, and replacing any assistive technology device.

Specific plans called "sensory diets" can be developed, typically by an occupational therapist, for individuals with sensory challenges. This term was introduced by Patricia Wilbarger in 1984 to describe how certain sensory experiences can improve occupational performance and may remediate the disruption of an individual's sensory systems (OT Innovations, 2018). These diets are activities that are scheduled into a student's day to help him or her regulate his or her activity levels. A sensory diet uses strategies and equipment that are practical, mindfully scheduled, and controlled to adjust an individual's sensory input. It is important that sensory diets be developed with careful thought on the timing, frequency, intensity, and duration of the sensory strategies. Some occupational therapists compare the use of a "sensory diet" to eating a well-balanced meal. To eat healthy, individuals eat a variety of foods from different food groups. A "sensory diet" works similarly by providing individuals with sensory challenges the variety of sensory input they need to function within their environment. Sensory diets are not just for individuals with identified sensory challenges. We all use a variety of sensory input to function appropriately within our environments. Our bodies instinctively seek or avoid sensory input without the use of sensory interventions.

What Is the Impact on Students in General Education?

In 2015, President Obama signed the Every Student Succeeds Act (ESSA) into law. ESSA was created to focus on fully preparing all students for success beyond high school and moving forward toward higher education and future careers by implementing efforts to close the achievement gap. Within ESSA, several references are made to the Universal Design for Learning (UDL), as defined in the Higher Education Opportunity Act of 2008 (CAST, 2016):

> "Universal Design for Learning (UDL) means a scientifically valid framework for guiding educational practice that—(A) provides flexibility in the ways information is presented, in the ways student respond or demonstrate knowledge and skills, and in the way students are engaged; and (B) reduces barriers in instruction, provides appropriate accommodations, supports, and challenges, and maintains high achievement expectations for all students, including students with disabilities and students who are limited English proficient."

The idea of universal design was originally applied to barrier-free design and architectural accessibility to ensure products and environments are usable by all people to the greatest extent possible without the need for adaptations. This approach has been applied to instructional practices with the intent to reduce the learning barriers for all students in educational environments. One concept UDL recognizes is that the learning space is an important component of the entire educational experience. A positive instructional climate can be created by considering the students' perceptions and effort, as well as the physical space and climate.

All students perceive information in a variety of ways, whether they have SPD, another disability, are gifted, or are a typically developing student. Some students prefer to utilize visual sensory input to gain information through silent reading and writing notes. Other students may find visual information overwhelming and prefer to utilize their auditory sensory input by listening to lectures or audio books. The UDL recommends providing students with instruction delivered in multiple forms to make the information equally accessible to all students.

The UDL also guides educators to maintain student alertness and reduce fatigue in the instructional environment by varying instruction and by including movement breaks between activities. This can also be done by arranging the physical environment to create movement during transitions as well as providing an area for movement within the classroom. Considering the amount of time students spend in school, it is no wonder why some students feel overwhelmed and fatigued. They need time and a space to appropriately manage their feelings and regulate their bodies. Too often practices that are intended for a specific population of students also seem to positively influence all students. Some schools that have incorporated sensory friendly environments have not only noticed a calming influence for students with IEPs or 504 plans, but also experience an overall positive climate in the classroom. Due to this overall positive influence, schools have incorporated more sensory approaches, strategies, and equipment in regular education classrooms.

It is established that all students process sensory input in different ways. Their sensory processing abilities and needs influence their classroom performance. Sensory friendly learning environments help all students perform better since the modifications support the natural learning process for every student. In other words, they have a universal effect. A meta-analysis by Worthen (2010) reviewed studies focused on answering the question "Do sensory-based intervention strategies implemented in the general education classroom setting result in improved attention and/or academic performance?" (p. 76). After reviewing 13 articles including participants with and without a developmental diagnosis, it seems such interventions may indeed improve student attention and performance. Additionally, these environments increase academic success, which can lead to higher levels of independence and confidence, improved behavior and mood, improved social skills, stronger coping and self-advocacy skills, great chances of post-secondary education, and gainful employment.

The sensory area is a semi-private, structured therapeutic space within the classroom containing a variety of equipment to help students calm and focus so they can be better prepared for learning and interacting with others. This area has a specific arrangement, equipment, and purpose, as described in a student's IEP or 504 plan and/or through a sensory diet. The sensory area should maintain these specifications to ensure safety and compliance with the law. The sensory area could be used by other students who do not have an IEP or 504 plan.

Just as in anything related to special education, developing the sensory area takes a team approach. Members of the IEP, which include the regular education teacher, special education teacher, occupational therapist, and the LEA, and may also include a physical therapist and/or assistive technology consultant, collaborate to purchase, assemble, arrange, and implement the sensory area. It is the occupational and/or the physical therapist's responsibility to train the regular and special education teachers on the proper equipment use and implementation of the sensory area. The regular and special education teachers have the responsibility of reporting any equipment wear and tear, whether certain strategies are no longer effective, or if new sensory related issues are observed.

The sensory area should be introduced within the first week of school, during the same time basic classroom rules and routines are developed. Classroom discussions are used to explain the possible reasons why a student may use the sensory area. Rules are established as to how one should access the sensory area, the behavior expectations while using it, and how to return to learning. Students need to know the intended use of each piece of equipment, how to use it appropriately, and how to put it away when they are finished. It is beneficial to explain to all students that the sensory area is not a playroom. It is not a way to avoid a task or activity they do not want to do. They must know the sensory area is always there and that they have access to it when they need it. However, they also must complete the task or activity they started prior to using the sensory area. Students should not be sent to the sensory area for acting out. This reinforces the student's thought that "if I act out in your classroom, I can go have fun in the sensory area." Positively reinforce students when they are following the rules of the sensory area. Once the rules for the sensory area are established, the teacher demonstrates and the students model the expected behaviors. Some teachers have found it beneficial to allow the students to explore the sensory area prior to implementing its use. The exploration activity reduces distractions and the occurrences of students using the sensory area out of curiosity rather than need. Taking the extra effort and time to instruct students on the purpose and expectations of the sensory area may seem like a daunting task at first. However, by establishing the sensory area as a designated area in the classroom, and over time, students will respect and appreciate the sensory area for its intended use. Just as the purpose of special education is to address individual goals and objectives to promote independence, a sensory area can help promote the independence for all students in the classroom by helping them regulate their own sensory and emotional needs.

Conclusion

In summary, people depend on several senses in their body to help gather information from the environment to perform daily activities. The way the nervous system receives input from one's senses and interprets the input into responses is called sensory processing. Everyone processes sensory input differently. Some individuals experience difficulties with processing sensory information, which is referred to as SPD. SPD is not recognized by the DSM-5 (APA, 2013) as a stand-alone diagnosis. This creates possible issues with the eligibility of special education services for students who experience sensory processing challenges. Students who have comorbid diagnosis, such as autism, are eligible for special education services to address their sensory processing needs. Students' sensory processing needs could also be addressed through Section 504 of the Rehabilitation Act of 1973. All students' sensory processing abilities influence their classroom performance. Research has shown that the implementation of a sensory friendly classroom not only positively impacts students with documented disabilities, but also similarly impacts all students. Sensory-friendly learning environments help all students perform better since the modifications support the natural learning process. In other words, sensory-friendly classrooms have a universal effect.

References

American Psychiatric Association. (2013). *Diagnostic and statistical manual of mental disorders* (5th ed.). Arlington, VA: American Psychological Association.

Arky, B. (2017). The debate over sensory processing: A look at the dispute over whether sensory symptoms constitute a disorder, and whether treatment works. *Child Mind Institute*. Retrieved from https://childmind.org/article/the-debate-over-sensory-processing/

Ben-Sasson, A., Carter, A. S., & Briggs Gowan, M. J. (2009). Sensory over-responsivity in elementary school: Prevalence and social-emotional correlates. *Journal of Abnormal Child Psychology, 37*(5), 705–716.

CAST. (2016, February 17). *UDL in the ESSA*. Retrieved from http://www.cast.org/whats-new/news/2016/udl-in-the-essa.html#.W79avWhKiM8

Centers for Disease Control and Prevention. (2016). Attention-deficit/hyperactivity disorder: Data & statistics. Retrieved from https://www.cdc.gov/ncbddd/adhd/data.html

Centers for Disease Control and Prevention. (2018). Prevalence of autism spectrum disorder among children aged 8 years-autism and developmental disabilities monitoring network, 11 sites, United States, 2014. *Surveillance Summaries, 67*(6), 1–23.

Levi-Shackleford, Z. (2015). *The effects of a sensory friendly learning environment on students with intellectual and developmental disabilities*. Retrieved from https://www.slideshare.net/ZipporahLeviShacklef/the-effects-of-a-sensory-friendly-learning-environment-on-students-with-intellectual-and-developmental-disabilities

Miller, L. J. (2014). Sensational kids: Hope and help for children with sensory processing disorder (2nd ed.). New York, NY: Perigee.

OT Innovations. (2018). *Sensory diets*. Retrieved from https://www.ot-innovations.com/clinical-practice/sensory-modulation/sensory-diets/.

Worthen, E. (2010). Sensory-based interventions in the general education classroom: A critical appraisal of the topic. *Journal of Occupational Therapy, Schools, & Early Intervention 3*(1), 76–94.

Wright, P. D., & Wright, P. D. (2017). *Special education law* (2nd ed.). Hartfield, VA: Harbor House Law Press, Inc.

EXTENSION ACTIVITIES

Discussion Questions

1. SPD is not a stand-alone diagnosis in the DSM-5 (APA, 2013). Do you think SPD should be a stand-alone diagnosis? If a person has a significantly impaired ability to interpret sensory information wouldn't they have a "disability" in a sense? What about the student who has sensory processing impairments but does not have a comorbid diagnosis and his or her sensory processing issues are not significant enough to fall under Section 504 of the Rehabilitation Act?
   a. Discuss how you would solve this problem if you were a school administrator.
   b. How will you ensure that you are addressing a student's needs and not putting your school district in legal jeopardy?
   c. Identify what laws you are abiding by or that are supporting your decisions.
2. How does a school district determine whether a sensory area is being used according to its intended use?
   a. Explain how you would determine this if you were the one making the decision.
3. Could a case be made for the implementation of sensory areas in all classrooms?
   a. Explain you answer.
4. Research the use of sensory areas in the classroom. Do the benefits of having a sensory-friendly environment in schools outweigh the potential disadvantages?
   a. Explain your answer.

Write a Letter Assignment

Pick a side:

Write a letter from a parent's view to your child's school administrator outlining the reasons why your child should have a sensory area in his or her regular education classroom.

Write a letter from a parent's view opposing having a sensory area located your child's classroom.

Discussion Paper

After reading this chapter, find a minimum of two additional articles that support this topic and write a double-spaced discussion paper following APA guidelines, including a bibliography page, to address the following within your paper:

- Before reading this chapter, my opinion on this issue was _____.

- In your own words, what is the issue at hand?

- Analyze what you see as the two sides of this issue.

- Identify a perceived misconception from either side. (When doing this, list the actual sentence(s) or portion of the sentence, citing the page number that you are making reference to, then write your response as to why you think it is a misconception. The key word is "perceived.")

- And finally, which side do you personally agree with more and why? (Refer to your personal experiences, here. If you have dealt with this issue in your personal life, work, teaching, etc., include that information in your answer.)

- Make sure to include in-text citations (when appropriate) from the supporting articles that you found.

Section II

Behavior

Chapter 3

Positive Behavior Intervention and Support (PBIS)
What Are the Benefits to Students and Teachers?

Eric Briggs

PICTURE THIS: It's late Friday afternoon and you have had a long week of teaching with your sixth-grade class. You just started the "bell ringer" to your next lesson in math when you notice one of the students in your class is chewing gum. You can hear the student chewing and so can other students in the classroom. You politely ask the student to throw the chewing gum into the garbage. The student complies as you briefly stop your instruction. As the student walks by you to the trash can, you hear the student say in a low voice, "this stupid teacher."

What Is the Issue?

One of the key functions of the public education system is to provide academic, social, and emotional support to all students who live within the boundaries of their school district. Because public school systems are unable to pick and choose who they educate, teachers are sometimes faced with students who exhibit challenging behaviors in the educational setting. How teachers choose to handle these challenging behavioral situations can have a drastic impact on the education of each child present in the classroom while the teacher is addressing the noncompliant child.

Positive behavior interventions and supports (PBIS) is an "implementation framework for maximizing the selection and use of evidence-based prevention and intervention practices along a multi-tiered continuum that supports the academic, social, emotional, and behavioral competence of all students (Office of Special Education Programs 2018, p. 1). The framework is based on four key implementation elements: data, outcomes, practices, and systems.

Students within the framework are identified as needing varying levels of behavioral support in their educational setting. Each level of support is called a tier. Students identify in one of three tiers of support. This is based on the level and need of support that the child needs to be successful in the educational setting. In order for the program to be successful, consistent implementation of the program must exist from the classroom to the district level; technical support and other professional learning opportunities should also be conducted from the local through the state level as a school system works through the different implementation phases of PBIS.

Being able to implement an effective PBIS program has challenges at many levels. Implementing inconsistencies between classrooms can hinder the behavioral growth of some of the most challenging students. Changes in leadership, prioritizing what the leader deems important to implementation, can lead to implementation of subsystems in the PBIS program. Finally, lack of a professional learning community that will sustain the program and hold the staff implementing the program accountable (through data-driven decisions) can also present issues for effective implementation at the classroom, building, and district level of PBIS.

Still today, school systems struggle to meet the behavioral and academic needs of the most challenging students. These students often have serious social and emotional issues, possess one or more mental health issues, and have multiple environmental factors that play a critical role in the decision-making process of the students. These students seem to live much of their life in a "fight-or-flight" mode when faced with some of life's simplest decisions.

What Does the Law Say?

During the 1980s a need was identified for educational systems to improve selection, implementation, and documentation of interventions used with students who have behavioral or conduct disorders (Sugai & Horner, 1999). Efforts to address this need were focused around preventive rather than reactive measures. Efforts indicated that greater attention should be directed toward prevention, research-based practices, data-based decision making, school-wide systems, explicit social skills instruction, team-based implementation and professional development, and student outcomes (Sugai & Horner, 2002).

During the 1990s, after a call for zero-tolerance policies arose, the federal government reauthorized the Individuals with Disabilities Education Act (IDEA) of 1997. Through this reauthorization, a grant was created to develop the National Center on Positive Behavior Interventions and Supports. This center was given the responsibility to provide technical assistance to schools on evidenced-based practices for improving supports on children with behavioral and conduct disorders (Sugai & Simonsen, 2012). IDEA is the only approach mentioned in the law, and furthermore, the laws have emphasis on using functional assessment and positive approaches to encourage good behavior for all students. Functional assessments provide critical data about students to assist educational professionals in making educational placement decisions for students.

With the reauthorization of IDEA in 2004, Congress explicitly recognized the potential of PBIS to prevent exclusion and improve educational results of students in all educational settings. In the passage of the Individuals with Disabilities Education Act (2004), Congress cited over 30 years of research on students with disabilities and how their education can be positively impacted when providing incentives for whole-school approaches, scientifically based early reading programs, positive behavioral interventions and supports, and early intervening services to reduce the need to label children as disabled in order to address the learning and behavioral needs of such children. Furthermore, when addressing the individualized education plan (IEP) of students whose behavior impedes their learning, IEP teams must always consider PBIS when addressing the behaviors of concern and conduct functional behavioral assessments to collect data around the behaviors impeding the child's learning.

How Does This Affect Schools?

As schools look to address the diverse academic, behavioral, social, and emotional needs that students bring into the classroom, challenges will always exist for school systems to meet all the needs of all the students. It is public schools' responsibility to offer a continuum of placement options for students who have such challenging needs. Because of this responsibility, school systems have to find effective ways to implement programs such as PBIS to meet student needs in the least restrictive environment possible.

In order to meet these diverse needs, school districts often have to look at how they can best allocate their resources so that the neediest children are receiving the most support. This can often be a challenge for districts, as school district may have to increase staffing due to the specific needs a child possesses. Therefore, an increase in expenditures could exist in specific programs, because the needs of a particular child are greater than perhaps his or her nondisabled peers.

The allocation of resources becomes even more of a challenge for administrators when attempting to meet the needs that gifted students or hard-working, high-achieving students bring to the classroom. These students often need very minimal structure and support to be successful in the classroom; however, they often also lose resources they once had because the reallocation of the resource was provided to students who have more challenging academic or behavioral needs in the same building or district. This is why it is often important for administrators to understand and communicate to the stakeholders the difference between equality and equity.

What Is the Impact on Students Needing Special Education or 504 Plan Services?

PBIS provides school systems with a framework on how to address the behavioral challenges students bring into the classroom. PBIS also provides IEP teams and 504 plan teams additional resources when looking at placement options for students with disabilities. These resources can become very valuable for IEP teams as they look at least restrictive educational options for students with disabilities.

Nondisabled students do not have the same additional rights that students with disabilities have through the passage of special education legislations since the early 1970s. Because of the additional rights that students with disabilities have, IEP and 504 plan teams must consider how student academic, behavioral, social, and emotional needs can be met in various educational placement settings. For example, all students are entitled to receive their education in a general education setting. This setting may include students with and without disabilities. Before other placement options can be considered, IEP teams must consider the supplementary aides and services that can be provided in that setting to support a child so they can be both academically and behaviorally successful in this setting. Only when all the supplementary aides and services have been exhausted should IEP teams look to consider other educational placements across the continuum.

PBIS provides additional resources and a framework for teachers to use as they look at the supplementary aids and services they can provide to such students in their general education classroom setting. For example, PBIS components such as a "check-in-check-out" system provide teachers the opportunity to have a dialogue with a child about how his or her day is going at various times throughout the school day. The principal's "100 Club" allows student to earn rewards as a positive reinforcer for those students who are caught "being good" throughout their time at school and receive a reward from their building principal. Finally, students are provided time to be retaught behaviors they are struggling with (those they struggle with by choice or those they have not been taught to perform) during embedded re-teaching times for students so they can correct their socially inappropriate behaviors and learn an alternative, more socially acceptable behavior as a replacement. These are just three of the most common types of behavioral reinforcements and interventions implemented in PBIS.

The educational placement outcomes of students with disabilities or 504 plans can often times look much different that they did 20 to 30 years ago. Therefore, this can create even more challenges for teachers who may not have had the professional learning opportunities through undergraduate or graduate programs to meet the academic and behavioral needs of students in the general education setting who exhibit challenging behaviors. PBIS provides teachers with a systematic, research-based approach on how to address and develop socially accepted behaviors for all students.

Teachers who may have taught or been educated in a zero-tolerance educational setting will often struggle with implementation at first. Educating the teachers on what PBIS is and is not is often the biggest challenge faced through the initial implementation stages of the program. For example, often time educators see this program as bribing students to get them to do what you want, or they believe that only students who exhibit challenging behaviors are rewarded for doing great things. What about the student who comes to school each day and does not need additional supports? How does this program benefit him or her? Often times, once the staff "buy into" the program, behavioral results of students will improve over time if the program is implemented with fidelity.

What Is the Impact on Students in General Education?

When implemented with fidelity, the goal of PBIS is to keep as many students as possible in the least restrictive education setting as possible. As a result, students who at one time received their educational services in more restrictive settings are now entitled to be in the general education setting if this setting is deemed to be the least restrictive environment for that child. How can the students and teachers be supported through PBIS in the general education classroom?

One of the key subsystems of PBIS is the development of rules. These rules, usually only three to five, are posted in every classroom, in the hallways, and in every location in a school building a child may visit. The rules are developed by a committee of teachers. Once the rules are developed, teachers are then taught how to take any behavior they may see in their classroom and tie it back to one of the three to five established school rules. For example, if a student calls another student a name and one of the school rules is to "act responsible," the name calling is then tied back to acting responsible and when the behavior intervention is discussed through the re-teaching process, the teacher will focus on how name calling is not responsible, and the teacher will also have the student cite evidence of how a student can act responsible (instead of name calling). As you can see, this provides teachers with a systematic approach to addressing behaviors. The approach to behavior remains the same whether the child has a diverse ability or does not.

PBIS allows for teachers to make systematic, data-driven decisions about the behaviors of all students. Behaviors are divided into two main categories, major or minor infractions. Major infractions are behavioral infractions that require the assistance of an administrator to address. Minor behavior fractions are those infractions that teachers in the classroom are expected to address in the classroom. All minor and major behavior fractions are defined by a team of teachers to assist their colleagues in differentiating whether the behavior is considered a major or a minor behavior. Minor behaviors, when they reach a certain criterion as established by the team, can become major behavioral infractions. Again, this threshold is predetermined by a committee of teaching staff.

As mentioned earlier, implementation of PBIS presents challenges. Some of these challenges require teachers to also change their behavior on how they address student misbehavior. Teachers can have a tendency to address misbehavior in ways that inadvertently reinforce the inappropriate behavior the student exhibits. This can occur when the teacher does not understand the function of the behavior (escape, avoid, attain, etc.). Not only are teachers equipped with interventions to address the socially unacceptable behaviors, but teachers are expected to "catch kids being good" in the academic setting. The goal is that other students will see that teachers acknowledge and support the socially acceptable behaviors and that other students, through reinforcement or teaching, will display the same behaviors as their peers.

Inevitably, there will be students who will be unable to be successful in a full general education setting because the supplementary aids and services provided in this setting will not be enough for them to attain academic or behavioral success. In these instances, students will look at an increased level of support, which may include smaller class size, paraprofessional support, or dedicated time for social skills training. These supports are often provided in more restrictive settings where students' needs can be more easily met. Because a change in educational placement is a process, students may exhibit inappropriate behaviors for a period of time before they are placed in a more restrictive setting. This is because all decisions based on student educational placement need to be data driven and a series of behavioral interventions need to be proven ineffective before the educational placement change can occur.

Conclusion

In conclusion, PBIS is a systematic approach based on research that supports educational entities in meeting the behavioral needs of all students in their educational institutions. PBIS was designed in a response to the passage of the IDEA 1997 legislation that called for technical assistance to schools on evidenced-based practices for improving supports for children with behavioral and conduct disorders. The framework has changed how public school systems address student misbehavior. When implemented with fidelity, PBIS is a research-based tool that provides concrete data for IEP and 504 plan teams to make educational placement decisions based on behavior so that all students can receive a free and appropriate public education in the least restrictive environment. PBIS is the one system that provides interventions and supports to teachers and students, and the core focus of PBIS is determining how data, outcomes, systems, and practices can positively impact all students so they can be productive members in their local, regional, and global communities.

References

Individuals with Disabilities Education Act 20 U.S.C. § 1401(c)(5)(F) (2004). Retrieved from https://www.pbis.org/school/pbis-and-the-law

Office of Special Education Programs. (2017). *What is school-wide PBIS?* Retrieved from https://www.pbis.org/school

Sugai, G., & Horner, R. H. (1999). Discipline and behavioral support: Preferred processes and practices. *Effective School Practices*, 17(4), 10–22.

Sugai, G., & Horner, R. H. (2002). The evolution of discipline practices: School-wide positive behavior supports. *Child and Family Behavior Therapy*, 24(1–2), 23–50.

Sugai, G., & Simonsen, B. (2012). Positive behavioral interventions and support: History, defining features, and misconceptions. *OSEP Technical Assistance Center on Positive Behavioral Interventions and Supports: Effective Schoolwide Interventions*. Retrieved from https://www.pbis.org/.../pbisresources/PBIS%20Part%201%2018%20Oct%202015%2...

EXTENSION ACTIVITIES

Discussion Questions

1. IDEA states that every child who attends a school district that receives federal funding is entitled to a free and appropriate public education in the least restrictive environment. This means that every child is entitled access, to some degree, to the regular education setting. It is the responsibility of the school district, and more specifically, in many cases, the IEP team, to determine how a child's academic, behavioral, and social emotional needs will be met in the educational environment. Knowing this to be true, consider the following questions:

   a. As a classroom teacher, how will you use what you know and understand about PBIS to lead a parent-teacher conversation with a parent of a child who is exhibiting disruptive behaviors in your classroom?

   b. As an administrator, a parent comes to your office to complain about the constant disruption of a student who is not responding to interventions and supports provided to a student who shares the same trigonometry classroom as his daughter. The daughter shares that the child constantly is yelling out answers, calling the teacher inappropriate names, and calling other students names. How will you handle the parent?

   c. You are tasked to present a 25- to 30-minute presentation to the public about how IDEA (special education), ADA (504 accommodations), and PBIS interrelate to ensure that all students can be successful in the educational environment. What are five to seven critical areas of focus you would use to develop this presentation?

2. How would you persuade a fellow teacher who believes in zero-tolerance polices for behavior to "buy into" the PBIS approach to addressing the behavioral needs of students?
3. You have been asked to develop a presentation on your school's Back to School Night that educates the parents about PBIS. What are some areas of PBIS you would focus on during this presentation?
4. Pretend you are going to bring parents into your classroom so they can see what PBIS "looks like" in the classroom. In essence, the parents are the students and you are the teacher. You are going to teach a school-wide lesson on the three to five behaviors your PBIS team has identified. What would this model lesson look like?

Write a Letter Assignment

5. You have been asked by your building administrator to write a letter to the local newspaper about the new educational framework your elementary school will be implementing in the upcoming school year: PBIS. Draft a letter to include the following:
   a. What is PBIS?
   b. What does the implementation process look like? How long does it take to fully implement the program?
   c. Define and describe the three tiers of support.
   d. Differentiate between PBIS and zero-tolerance policies and why PBIS is a more effective behavioral intervention than zero-tolerance approaches.

Discussion Paper

After reading this chapter, find a minimum of three additional articles that support PBIS and write a double-spaced discussion paper following APA guidelines, including a reference page, to address the following:

- Before reading the chapter, what was your opinion of PBIS?

- In your own words, describe whether you would support the implementation of PBIS in your local school.

- Identify and describe what you believe are the top three critical elements when implementing the PBIS framework.

- Identify two to three perceived misconceptions about PBIS. (When doing this, list the actual sentence(s) or portion of the sentence, citing the page number that you are making reference to, then write your response as to why you think it is a misconception.) The key word is "perceived.")

- Make sure to include in-text citations (when appropriate) from the supporting articles that you found.

Chapter 4

Crisis Management
How Should Schools Support Students if They are Engaging in Dangerous Behavior?

Edward G. Nientimp

PICTURE THIS: A new student has just moved into your school district and is placed in your fourth-grade classroom. You are aware that he has a history of abuse and has had multiple placements at residential treatment facilities. When Mac has trouble unzipping his jacket you try to assist him, and he immediately yells "stop hurting me" and proceeds to scratch you and attempts to bite you. You try to redirect him, but he continues to try to hurt you. The teacher across the hall hears what is happening and observes you trying to keep Mac from hurting you while he is hysterically screaming, kicking, and scratching. The teacher puts Mac into a hold and restrains him.

What Is the Issue?

Starting in the mid-1970s all students with disabilities have been guaranteed the right to attend public school programs in the least restrictive environment. All students, even those students with severe emotional and behavioral challenges, have the expectation of receiving a free and appropriate public school education. Prior to the Individuals with Disabilities Education Act (IDEA), students with significant behavioral challenges were frequently excluded from public school. Students who engaged in behaviors that were dangerous to themselves or others were more likely to be kept at home or at best attend school at a residential program or psychiatric center. This all changed with the IDEA, which opened the door to all students, including those with challenging behavior (Ryan & Peterson, 2004; Ryan, Robbins, Peterson, & Rozalski, 2009).

Using restraint (holding a student so that he or she is not able to freely move) is a controversial subject. Restraint is a common component of most crisis management packages. The use of restraint has been debated in adult settings (geriatric care, psychiatric hospitals, residential settings) for 250 years. It is a relatively new phenomenon in public school settings. In 2009 multiple reports acted as a lightning rod that captured the attention of the federal government (Council of Parent Attorneys and Advocates, 2009; Duncan, 2009; National Disabilities

Rights Network, 2009; U.S. Government Accountability Office, 2009). In its report titled "School is Not Supposed to Hurt," the National Disabilities Rights Network (2009) chronicled incidents of restraint and abuse occurring at schools in almost all 50 states, including multiple examples where students died in the hands of school staff who were restraining them. The United States Government Accountability Office (GAO) reported 24 restraint or seclusion deaths in the prior year that occurred in schools providing services for students with disabilities (GAO, 2009). The report of 24 deaths was thought to be an underestimation of restraint-related deaths due to the poor systems for data collection employed at that time (Sturmey, 2015). The GAO (2009) report cited significant challenges in providing oversight to restraint use in schools due to a lack of federal regulations. Subsequent investigation and reporting resulted in 15 recommendations (U.S. Department of Education, 2012), which have the strength of guidance but fall short of a law or regulation. The intent of the GAO was to inform state policy and provide guidance for regulatory controls regarding the use of restraint (Marx & Baker, 2017). There has been increased concern and public outcry regarding restraint utilization with children attending school (U.S. Department of Education, 2012).

The U.S. Department of Education (DOE), in a response to a directive from the then Director of Education Arne Duncan, concluded that "restraint or seclusion should not be used as routine school safety measures; that is, they should not be implemented except in situations where a child's behavior poses imminent danger of serious physical harm to self or others and not as a routine strategy implemented to address instructional problems or inappropriate behavior (e.g., disrespect, noncompliance, insubordination, out of seat), as a means of coercion or retaliation or as a convenience" (U.S. Department of Education, 2012, p. 3).

We know that students with self-injurious behavior and aggressive behavior are attending public schools. Despite many schools adopting school-wide positive behavior supports and having greater capacity to implement individualized behavior programs that are based on functional analysis of behavior, there still is potential that a student may engage in behavior that presents a clear and present danger to him- or herself or to others. When all the positive, research-based interventions are unsuccessful, should school staff utilize a physical management technique (restraint) to hold a student until he or she is calm?

What Does the Law Say?

There are no federal laws governing restraint. In 2012 the United States Department of Education issued 15 guidelines for schools to follow. The guidelines state, among other things, "[T]hat restraint should be used if the behavior poses imminent danger of serious physical harm to self or others; that restraint or seclusion should never be used as punishment or discipline; [that] restraint or seclusion should never be used in a manner that restricts a child's breathing; and that behavior strategies should be used to address underlying causes of dangerous behavior" (U.S. Department of Education, 2012, pp. 12–13).

Marx and Baker (2017) reviewed state legislation and policy to determine how closely each state was ascribing to the guidelines established by the Department of Education. Thirty-eight states have regulations or statutes that govern the use of restraint in schools. These laws are largely based on the federal guidelines. One such example of a state statue would be the state of Pennsylvania's Public School Code (22 PA Code §14.133 et seq., 2007) which gives school districts very clear guidance regarding the use of restraint. The school code includes definitions as to what is considered a restraint and what is considered necessary physical support for students. The school code describes that students may not be restrained in a face-down (prone) position and that restraints may only be used when a student is acting in a manner as to be a clear and present danger to him- or herself or to other students or employees, and only when less restrictive measures and techniques have proven to be or are less effective.

Most school districts have a policy that describes what is permissible at the district level. These policies are frequently found under titles such as behavior management, use of reasonable force, or crisis management.

How Does This Affect Schools?

School districts must adopt policies and develop strategic plans so that they are able to support all students. Students who may engage in behaviors that are dangerous to themselves or others will require that teachers and/or ancillary staff are capable of properly supporting students should their behavior become escalated.

It should be assumed that schools have in place positive behavior support plans focused on replacement skill development for students with behavioral challenges. Once the function of a behavior is identified, IEP teams should develop a comprehensive behavior plan that will target replacement skills for the challenging behavior. Most behavior plans look to modify antecedent conditions or triggers to make sure the behavior is less likely to occur, while at the same time developing positive reinforcement when the student engages in the replacement behavior. Despite having these positive practices in place, some students may continue to engage in negative patterns of behavior that may be dangerous.

The dilemma is real. How does a district respond to a crisis when a student is engaging in behavior that is dangerous to him- or herself or others, knowing that restraint has been shown to have a negative impact on students, including injury and trauma (Amos, 2004; Azeem, Reddy, Wudarsky, Carabetta, Gregory, & Sarofin, 2015). School districts must adopt policies that clearly give frontline staff direction and training in how to handle these challenging situations.

A common approach for many school districts is to purchase a crisis management training package from a private vendor. A recent study identified that there are 25 vendors who market a product that is geared toward crisis intervention (Couvillon, Kane, Peterson, Ryan, & Scheuermann, 2018). The authors were able to compare 17 of the vendor programs and found that most offered (a) a didactic training for staff about crisis in general and students with disabilities, (b) verbal de-escalation training, (c) restraint procedures, and (d) debriefing strategies.

Some school districts are considering how many adult psychiatric centers and residential facilities have addressed crisis situations while trying to reduce or eliminate the need to restrain students. Huckshorn (2008) identified six principles that are common themes in research studies that have been effective in reducing or eliminating restraint and seclusion. The keys to reducing restraint were (a) administrative support, (b) debriefing methods, (c) staff training, (d) use of data to make decisions, (e) positive proactive behavioral approaches, and (f) parent or consumer involvement. Administrative support is when a school district administrator creates policy and procedures that provide direction to frontline staff. This is a top-down approach and crucial to the implementation of a district-wide program. Debriefing occurs after a crisis or behavioral episode has occurred. Staff involved in the incident are given an opportunity to review what happened with an administrator or supervisor to identify what went well, any challenges, and how to improve should a similar incident happen again. When appropriate, and when emotionally regulated, students may also discuss the incident with staff involved. Critical to the implementation of restraint-reduction efforts is staff development. Frontline teachers and support staff must be trained not only in the school's philosophy but also in trauma-informed care, causes and signs of student escalation, and finally the use of de-escalation strategies. School districts should have in place a system to collect data about student behavioral challenges and incidents of aggression or self-injury. Data-informed decisions should be made to support current approaches or identify needs for change. Positive behavior support is a critical component for any student with behavioral challenges. The importance of learning new skills and behaviors to replace those of concern are critical in eliminating problem behaviors. The literature is rich in examples of positive behavioral approaches that have led to the reduction of problem behavior and the development of replacement behavior (Cooper, Heron, & Heward, 2007).

One school district employed many of these principles to eliminate the use of restraint by implementing a licensed program called UKERU, which involved staff training in trauma-informed care and the use of soft blocking pads to extend the opportunity for intervention/

de-escalation as opposed to the use of restraint (Nientimp, 2018). In this example, school district administrators developed a policy that required all frontline staff to be trained in trauma-informed care and de-escalation techniques. Debriefing occurred after every student incident to support staff during program implementation. Ongoing restraint data over time clearly demonstrated that the use of restraint was replaced by de-escalation and soft blocking pads were used to support students while they were in crisis.

School districts must consider this very sensitive issue, chart a path or invest in a program, and then provide staff development and training so that frontline teachers and assistants are able to meet the behavioral challenges of their students in a safe and supportive manner.

What Is the Impact on Students Needing Special Education?

Most students who are eligible and in need of special education will never need to have a crisis plan. About 1% of all special education students will need this level of support due to behavior that is dangerous to themselves or others (Pennsylvania Department of Education, 2017). Some might believe that since this is such a small percentage of students it may not be worth the effort involved. Using Pennsylvania as an example, the entire state population of students receiving special education in the 2016–2017 school year was 283,145 and the number of students restrained was 4,373. That is 4,000-plus incidents that might end in injury, death, or result in trauma.

Crisis management that involves restraint takes a toll on the students who are restrained and the staff who are involved in the restraint. Most students and staff alike report that they do not like being restrained for obvious reasons. No teacher goes into the profession of education thinking that he or she may need to hold a student who is dangerous to him- or herself or others. Restraints can also result in litigation, missed work/school time for staff or students who are injured, and lead to teacher burnout.

What Is the Impact on Students in General Education?

When students engage in behavior that is dangerous to themselves (self-injury) or others (aggression such as hitting or biting), it frequently causes a disruption to the learning environment. Common approaches in an escalated student in a general education setting might be (a) having the students evacuate the room, which results in lost educational time and disruption to the routine; (b) having a crisis team enter the room to remove a student, which results in a major classroom disruption and potential embarrassment for the student in crisis. It is important to understand that these approaches may be confusing or disturbing for classmates to observe. It is not a common occurrence for most students to witness a peer that is dysregulated and may be acting out against classmates or the teacher is not a common occurrence for most students to witness.

Some students who have a history or tendency to engage in disruptive behavior may be taught in a more self-contained classroom (a special education classroom where all students have an individualized education plan). While student escalation in a self-contained setting may seem to have less impact on the general education setting, there are indirect effects. School administrators and support staff are frequently called to classrooms when there is a significant incident, thus taking away from their ability to attend to general education responsibilities.

Conclusion

There are students attending public schools who will need external supports when they engage in behavior that is dangerous to themselves (such as self-injury) or to others (such as aggression). School districts must develop policies and clear guidelines that all staff are aware of so that they are prepared to deal with a crisis. School administrators must balance the safety of the students and staff with their mandate to support students in the least restrictive environment. Many school districts purchase commercial training programs and make sure that frontline staff have adequate training in verbal de-escalation and restraint training so that they can safely support a student in crisis. There are other crisis management approaches that do not employ a restraint and focus more on taking a trauma-informed care approach. Soft blocking shields are used to keep staff and students safe during the crisis.

References

Amos, P. A. (2004). New considerations in the prevention of aversives, restraint, and seclusion: Incorporating the role of relationships into an ecological perspective. *Research and Practice for Persons with Severe Disabilities, 29*(4), 263–272. doi:10.2511/rpsd.29.4.263

Azeem, M. W., Reddy, B., Wudarsky, M., Carabetta, L., Gregory, F., & Sarofin, M. (2015). Restraint reduction at a pediatric psychiatric hospital: A ten-year journey. *Journal of Child and Adolescent Psychiatric Nursing, 28*(4), 180–184.

Cooper, J. O., Heron, T. E., & Heward, W. L. (2007). *Applied behavior analysis* (2nd ed.). Upper Saddle River, NJ: Pearson/Merrill-Prentice Hall.

Council of Parent Attorneys and Advocates (2009). *Unsafe in the schoolhouse: Abuse of children with disabilities.* Towson, MD: Author

Couvillon, M. A., Kane, E. J., Peterson, R. L., Ryan, J. B., & Scheuermann, B. (2018). Policy and Program Considerations for Choosing Crisis Intervention Programs. *Journal of Disability Policy Studies*, 1–11.

Duncan, A. (2009, July 31). *Letter to chief state school officers.* Retrieved from http://www2.ed.gov//policy/elsec/guid/secletter/090731.html

Huckshorn, K. A. (2008). Six core strategies for reducing seclusion and restraint use planning tool. *National Association of State Mental Health Program Directors.* Retrieved from www.nasmhpd.org

Marx, T. A., & Baker, J. N. (2017). Analysis of restraint and seclusion legislation and policy across states: Adherence to recommended principles. *Journal of Disability Policy Studies, 28*(1), 23–31. doi:10.1177/1044207317702069

National Disability Rights Network (2009). School is not supposed to hurt: The U.S. Department of Education must do more to protect school children from restraint and seclusion. *National Disability Rights Network.* Retrieved from http://www.ndrn.org/images/Documents/Resources/Publications/Reports/School_is_Not_Supposed_to_Hurt_3_v7.pdf

Nientimp, E. (2018). *The effects of staff training in blocking techniques and trauma informed care on the number of student restraints in a special education setting at a suburban public school district* (Unpublished doctoral dissertation). Slippery Rock University, Slippery Rock, PA.

Ryan, J. B., Peterson, R. L., Tetreault, G., & van der Hagen, E. (2008). Reducing the use of seclusion and restraint in a day school program. In M. A. Nunno, D. M. Day, & L. B. Bullard (Eds.), *For our own safety: Examining the safety of high-risk interventions for children and young people* (pp. 201–215). Arlington, VA: Child Welfare League of America.

Ryan, J. B., Robbins, K., Peterson, R., & Rozalski, M. (2009). Review of state policies concerning the use of physical restraint procedures in schools. *Education and Treatment of Children, 32*(3), 487–504. doi:10.1353/etc.0.0062

Sturmey, P. (2015). *Reducing restraint and restrictive behavior management practices.* New York, NY: Springer.

U.S. Department of Education (2012). Restraint and seclusion: Resource document. Washington, DC: Author. Retrieved from http://www.ed.gov/policy/restraintseclusion

U.S. Government Accountability Office, 1999. *Report to Congressional Requesters: Mental Health: Improper Restraint or Seclusion Use Places People at Risk.* Retrieved from http://www.gao.gov/assets/230/228149.pdf

EXTENSION ACTIVITIES

Discussion Questions

1. Students with disabilities have the right to receive a free appropriate public education in the least restrictive environment (LRE).

a. What does LRE mean for a student who engages in behavior that is dangerous to him- or her-self (such as self-injury) or to others (such as aggression)?

b. Explain what you would do if you had a student move into your district who engaged in aggressive behavior toward a teacher. What would you do during the crisis? What would you say to the parent? What would your plan be for the next school day?

c. Describe what sections of a student's IEP would address challenging behaviors such as aggression or self-injury and then give examples or what types of specially designed instruction or related services might be appropriate.

2. Review two different crisis management commercial programs.

a. Create a chart that compares the two training platforms.

b. Identify the program that you would select for your school staff and explain why you chose it.

3. Review a local school district policy and compare it with the U.S. Department of Education recommendations. Does the school district permit restraint? If the school district permits restraint, what are the parameters or requirements?

4. Interview a teacher or school district special education supervisor.

a. Find out how many restraints occurred at his or her school district last year.

b. Ask how they deal with students who are engaging in behavior that is dangerous.

c. How does the school district inform parents and support teachers?

d. Analyze the district's approach and identify any suggestions you might have for improvement.

5. Develop a position paper outlining a proposal that would help reduce the number of restraints being utilized at a school district. Consider utilizing UKERU as a "restraint-free" staff development program that might be used in place of traditional restraint training.

Write a Letter Assignment

Pick a side:

Write a letter to your school board of directors or school superintendent that supports a crisis management platform and the limited use of restraint.

Write a letter to your school board of directors or school superintendent that opposes the use of restraint entirely. Be prepared to give the board or superintendent acceptable alternatives.

Discussion Paper

After reading this chapter, find a minimum of two additional articles that support this topic and write a double-spaced discussion paper following APA guidelines, including a bibliography page, to address the following:

- Before reading this chapter, my opinion on this issue was _____.

- In your own words, what is the issue at hand?

- Analyze what you see as the two sides of this issue.

- Identify a perceived misconception from either side. (When doing this, list the actual sentence(s) or portion of the sentence, citing the page number that you are making reference to, then write your response as to why you think it is a misconception. The key word is "perceived.")

- And finally, which side do you personally agree with more and why? (Refer to your personal experiences, here. If you have dealt with this issue in your personal life, work, teaching, etc., include that information in your answer.)

- Make sure to include in-text citations (when appropriate) from the supporting articles that you found.

Chapter 5

Classroom Management
How Does the Lack of Classroom Management Training Impact Students in Early Childhood Classrooms?

Cybill Reed

> **PICTURE THIS:** You are a first-year teacher in an early childhood classroom teaching 17 children 3 to 5 years of age. You immediately start to notice that some of the children yell, hit, and even swear to get their wants and needs communicated. While you have done the basic tasks of setting up a classroom schedule and creating activities for diverse learners, you quickly realize that you have not been trained in how to deal with such diverse disruptive behaviors.

What Is the Issue?

As early childhood classrooms become more diverse and additional expectations are anticipated of teachers, classroom management has become a significant issue in relation to how teachers manage disruptive behaviors in their classroom. Early childhood classrooms are often the first chance a child has at learning routines and rules in a structured setting (Ersozlu & Cayci, 2016). Therefore, it is imperative that a child's first experience with discipline be done in a way that helps the child grow while learning his or her physical and social boundaries. While there are hundreds of strategies to use to manage students' disruptive behaviors in a classroom, knowing when and how to use those strategies has become a main topic for pre-service and first-year teachers.

While pre-service teachers are expected to know how to implement curriculum and have developed strong people skills when they leave college, those two skills alone will not create an effective teacher in the classroom. Pre-service teacher training programs often fail to prepare teachers to manage their classroom in an effective and efficient manner (MacSuga & Simonsen, 2011). Teachers in today's schools need to be able to manage a variety of behaviors while following strict curriculum guidelines. Pre-service teachers are simply given a review of different types of proactive classroom management techniques that might be useful to use in the classroom without ever having the opportunity to truly implement classroom management techniques. There is a significant difference between reading about proactive classroom management strategies and knowing how and when to implement those strategies in the classroom.

While pre-service programs need to focus on teaching evidence-based classroom management strategies, that need continues for teachers who are already employed in early childhood classrooms. When early childhood teachers experience high levels of stress, their ability to engage in a warm, responsive classroom greatly diminishes. This can result in an overemphasis on managing negative behaviors rather than providing an enriching and engaging classroom (Ritblatt, Honkoda, & Van Liew, 2017). Therefore, it becomes even more imperative that early childhood teachers continue to receive training in how to manage disruptive behaviors in their classrooms throughout their years of service.

Disruptive behaviors in preschool students can predict lower academic outcomes, motivation, attention, persistence, and attitude toward school (Ritz, Noltemeyer, & Green, 2014). In addition, early childhood educators describe dealing with disruptive behaviors as their main stressor (Ritblatt et al., 2017). When teachers are more prepared to manage disruptive behaviors by receiving adequate training, the early childhood environment becomes a positive learning atmosphere where children and teachers all succeed.

What Does the Law Say?

While there are laws governing the duration of pre-service teachers' teaching placements, there are no laws governing what type of experience pre-service teachers have in those classrooms. Some students may have the advantage of working with a seasoned teacher who uses the most current research in managing student behavior, while another student may be placed with a teacher who demonstrates very poor classroom management skills. Those two experiences can greatly shape how that teacher will manage his or her classroom during his or her first year of teaching. There is also no law mandating what type of continuing education hours are required for teachers. Continuing education hours can focus on classroom management, but they can also focus on learning about pre-kindergarten standards, how to physically arrange a classroom, or how to use specific curriculums. While all those topics are important, they do not specifically assist in how to manage disruptive behaviors in an early childhood classroom.

There are also no laws specifying what type of classroom management techniques and strategies have to be used in an early childhood setting. While trainings and schools often reference using "best practices" in relation to classroom management, that is a very vague term that can vary greatly from school to school and even classroom to classroom. It then becomes the responsibility of the classroom teacher to determine what "best practices" should be used in his or her classroom and how those strategies and techniques should be implemented.

Laws in education often govern specific needs of students and the standards to which teachers must adhere to remain state-certified teachers. However, since there are no laws governing how teachers manage their classroom, teachers are often left to determine classroom management strategies based on their personal experiences in school or from fellow teachers. While sometimes that can lead to strong classroom management skills, often it leads to teachers feeling inadequate in their ability to manage their classroom.

How Does This Affect Schools?

Poor classroom management skills affect schools, students, families, and teachers. As teachers find it more difficult to manage disruptive behaviors, they begin to develop a negative attitude towards their work environment. Zhang and Zeller (2016) found in their study that 40–50% of teachers will leave the classroom within their first 5 years and 9.5% will leave before the end of their first year of teaching. Their study also noted that a lack of classroom control was a major reason for teachers leaving the profession.

Teacher retention is an important topic in relation to classroom management because it can cause instability in the classrooms, increase student behaviors, and can create a negative learning environment. If the teacher does not want to be in the classroom, then the students will not either. When teacher turnover is high, students are not able to develop positive relationships with teachers that could in turn decrease disruptive behaviors. This is especially important in the early childhood setting.

Many early childhood settings have now adopted the use of positive behavior interventions and supports (PBIS) to help manage disruptive behaviors. PBIS is a community-based intervention that involves administrators, teachers, students, and families (Carr et al., 2002). It is not a concept to be used only with students with disabilities, but a program that, when used correctly, can increase the quality of learning outcomes while preventing problem behavior in all students (Sugai & Horner, 2002). Instead of teachers focusing on negative or disruptive behaviors, teachers focus on acknowledging students for appropriate behaviors. A major benefit of schools incorporating PBIS is the fact that each school can individualize the approach used and train teachers based on previous knowledge of classroom management skills, and PBIS integrates many other research-based classroom management strategies within the overall concept.

The additional benefit of using an approach like PBIS is that it is three tiered to incorporate all students. The OSEP Technical Assistance Center describes the hierarchy as follows: The first tier focuses on universal interventions that are for all students and are preventive and proactive in nature. The second tier focuses on secondary interventions for at-risk students, which includes high efficiency and rapid response to behaviors. The third tier focuses on tertiary interventions for individual students. These interventions are assessment based, intense, and durable procedures.

Many colleges are now incorporating classes into their teaching curriculum that focus on teaching pre-service teachers the basics of PBIS and how it should be implemented in the field of teaching. For teachers already in the field, there are numerous continuing education classes that focus solely on PBIS and how to create a more positive learning atmosphere. However, many pre-service early childhood teachers still do not receive the opportunity to utilize PBIS in their student teaching placements because of their cooperating teaching not being properly trained in PBIS. As for teachers in early childhood classrooms, teachers continue to report that going to trainings about PBIS and having coaches demonstrate how it could be incorporated into their classroom are two entirely different things.

Early childhood agencies are now hiring PBIS coaches to help go into the early childhood classrooms and model how PBIS should be incorporated into the daily routine. Research has proven that teaching expectations to young children, when they are enrolled in programs such as Head Start, can cause a proactive prevention that focuses on promoting social-emotional development; supporting the use of adaptive, pro-social behaviors; and preventing challenging behaviors (Carter & Pool, 2012). In addition, these coaches can address specific behavioral concerns with students in an early childhood classroom and give overall suggestions to make the learning environment more positive.

However, some early childhood centers are still unable to effectively incorporate PBIS into their classroom. This can be due to many reasons including teachers not wanting to change their method of classroom management, lack of funding for specialized PBIS coaches, and geographical locations of early childhood classrooms. Steed, Pomerleau, Muscott, and Rohde (2013) researched the challenges to implementing PBIS in rural early childhood settings. They found that the geographically large service area, lack of well-qualified and/or sufficient personnel, a scarcity of technological equipment or resources, increased costs of service delivery, and the compounding issue of increased poverty in rural areas has greatly impacted the ability for PBIS to be used with consistency and fidelity. PBIS in rural areas is often done with minimal hands-on training and without realistic expectations set by early childhood centers.

Using PBIS in early childhood settings must be specifically taught and followed through by early childhood agencies. PBIS works in all urban and rural areas, but rural areas may have a more difficult time training their teachers due to a lack of available trainings and resources. Therefore, it becomes vital that early childhood schools and agencies start to research how they can continue to train their teachers in developing strong classroom management skills.

What Is the Impact on Students Needing Special Education or 504 Plan Services?

Having teachers adequately trained in positive ways to manage disruptive behaviors becomes imperative when working with students with special needs. Research has found that 10.4% of state-funded pre-kindergarten teachers across the nation expelled at least one preschooler from their program during the 2003–2004 school year. One 2016 study found that 42% of all early childhood centers expel at least one child each year (Preventing Suspensions and Expulsions in Early Childhood Settings, 2016). This rate is astronomical when it is 3.2 times higher than the rate for kindergarten through 12th-grade children (Gebbie, Ceglowski, Taylor, & Miels, 2012).

Having teachers trained in how to manage disruptive behaviors would greatly decrease the number of early childhood students who are expelled from school. It is critical to remember that how a child views school, relationships with teachers, and relationships with peers is all shaped during a child's early childhood experience. Since disabilities such as autism, speech and language impairments, and intellectual disability are often diagnosed between the ages of 3 and 5 years of age, early childhood teachers need to know how to better serve these students in a typical early childhood classroom setting.

When behaviors such as yelling, swearing, and hitting become too much for early childhood teachers to handle, they often refer the child for special education. However, often the child is displaying age-appropriate behaviors that might just be more intense than other children their age. Instead of teachers trying to manage the behaviors within the classroom using research-based methods, they often refer the child for special education services because they are simply not trained in how to manage these behaviors.

Instead of an early childhood teacher referring a child for special education as soon as behaviors start to increase, that teacher needs to be trained in how to track the behaviors to look for patterns and antecedents that could cause these behaviors to happen. While some early childhood students may in fact need a more specialized setting, often times they need a teacher who has been trained in how to manage behaviors in a positive and caring manner.

In addition, with the increase of students with special needs being included in the general education setting, teachers need to learn appropriate developmental ways to manage a young child's behavior. It is no longer acceptable to simply allow the student to just leave the room, have a personal aide, or call the parent to take the student home when disruptive behaviors occur. Instead, the shift has been for teachers to begin to model appropriate behaviors, ignore inappropriate behaviors, and positively reinforce all students in the classroom. While this may sound like a simple solution, many teachers report that they feel they have received a lack of training in how to implement these types of strategies.

What Is the Impact on Students in General Education?

In early childhood classrooms, students displaying disruptive behaviors are not immediately taught in a separate setting but included in the general education setting daily. Thus, students who are displaying typical behavior in an early childhood classroom are often exposed to students who are hitting, yelling, or even swearing at teachers and other students. Therefore, it becomes imperative that early childhood teachers have a strong ability to manage their classroom environment.

Head Starts and pre-K classrooms often have between 13 and 17 students per classroom. There is always a teacher and a teacher assistant in the classroom. In best-case scenarios there is an additional teacher assistant to help in the classroom as well. However, when teachers are not trained properly in managing disruptive behaviors, one student displaying disruptive behaviors can quickly turn into 13 to 17 students displaying a range of disruptive behaviors.

Children between the ages of 3 to 5 years of age often learn behaviors from what they see and hear. This is where teachers being taught how to properly implement PBIS strategies becomes critical. Focusing on students who are making positive behavior choices will in turn help the students who are having disruptive behaviors. When an early childhood classroom is running with strong classroom management skills, the general education students become great models for students with more difficult behaviors. This also leads to children with disruptive behaviors being allowed to remain within the typical early childhood classroom.

Having any student with special needs or a student just displaying disruptive behaviors will require more work from the teacher. The teacher will need to learn how to properly reinforce positive and negative behaviors without the negative behaviors becoming the focal point of the classroom. Teachers will also have to teach the students how to ignore behaviors from other children while not making a child with special needs or disruptive behaviors feel like he or she is not part of the classroom.

Conclusion

In summary, having early childhood teachers receive additional and specific trainings in how to manage disruptive behaviors is a critical component to teacher retention and creating a positive classroom environment. It is important to remember that children between the ages of 2 and 5 represent a significant period of development. Unaddressed or negatively addressed behavioral problems during the preschool years can often lead to larger-scale social and behavioral difficulties later in life (Ritz et al., 2014). Despite the numerous evidence-based classroom management techniques available for early childhood educators to use in their classrooms, many teachers still use strategies that are not evidence-based or proactive in nature due to a lack of training and confidence in their ability to manage disruptive behaviors (Anderson & Kincaid, 2005; Carr et al., 2002). By teachers and schools focusing on preventing disruptive behaviors at an early age, the likelihood of problem behavior occurring will decrease. Children can only thrive in classrooms when there is consistency, predictability, and positivity (Carter & Pool, 2012).

References

Anderson, C. M., & Kincaid, D. (2005). Applying behavior analysis to school violence and discipline problems: Schoolwide positive behavior support. *Behavior Analyst, 28*(1), 49–63.

Carr, E. G., Dunlap, G., Horner, R. H., Koegel, R. L., Turnbull, A. P., Sailor, W., & Fox, L. (2002). Positive behavior support: evolution of an applied science. *Journal of Positive Behavior Interventions, 4*(1), 4–16.

Carter, D. R., & Pool, J. L. (2012). Appropriate social behavior: teaching expectations to young children. *Early Childhood Education Journal, 40*(5), 315–321.

Ersozlu, A., & Cayci, D. (2016). The changes in experienced teachers' understanding towards classroom management. *Universal Journal of Educational Research, 4*(1), 144–150.

Gebbie, D., Ceglowski, D., Taylor, L., & Miels, J. (2012). The role of teacher efficacy in strengthening classroom support for preschool children with disabilities who exhibit challenging behaviors. *Early Childhood Education Journal, 40*(1), 35–46.

MacSuga, A. S., & Simonsen, B. (2011). Increasing teachers' use of evidence-based classroom management strategies throughout consultation: Overview and case studies. *Beyond Behavior, 20*(2), 4–12.

Preventing Suspensions and Expulsions in Early Childhood Settings. (2016). *Overview.* Retrieved from https://preventexpulsion.org/overview/

Ritz, M., Noltemeyer, A., & Green, J. (2014). Behavior management in preschool classrooms: Insights revealed through systematic observation and interview. *Psychology in The Schools, 51*(2), 181–197.

Ritblatt, S. N., Hokoda, A., & Van Liew, C. (2017). Investing in the early childhood mental health workforce development: Enhancing professionals' competencies to support emotion and behavior regulation in young children. *Brain Sciences, 7*(9), 1–19.

Steed, E. A., Pomerleau, T., Muscott, H., & Rohde, L. (2013). Program-wide positive behavioral interventions and supports in rural preschools. *Rural Special Education Quarterly, 32*(1), 38–46.

Sugai, G., & Horner, R. H. (2002). Introduction to the special series on positive behavior support in schools. *Journal of Emotional & Behavioral Disorders, 10*(3), 130–235.

Zhang, G., & Zeller, N. (2016). A longitudinal investigation of the relationship between teacher preparation and teacher retention. *Teacher Education Quarterly, 43*(2), 73–92.

EXTENSION ACTIVITIES

Discussion Questions

1. Describe the classroom management preparation you have received and explain if you feel it has or has not adequately prepared you for working with students with disruptive behaviors.
2. Imagine that you have a student who is displaying disruptive behaviors (e.g., hitting, yelling, swearing); explain how the use of PBIS would assist you in managing those behaviors.
3. What do you feel is the biggest barrier to early childhood teachers using PBIS in their classrooms? Explain your answer.

Write a Letter Assignment

Pick a side:

Write a letter from a teacher's point of view on why a child with disruptive behaviors should be removed from the early childhood classroom and placed elsewhere.

Write a letter from a parent's view of why his or her child should be allowed to remain in the early childhood classroom regardless of disruptive behaviors.

Discussion Paper

After reading this chapter, find a minimum of two additional articles that support this topic and write a double-spaced discussion paper following APA guidelines, including a bibliography page, to address the following:

- Before reading this chapter, my opinion on this issue was _____.
- In your own words, what is the issue at hand?
- Analyze what you see as the two sides of this issue.
- Identify a perceived misconception from either side. (When doing this, list the actual sentence(s) or portion of the sentence citing the page number that you are making reference to, then write your response as to why you think it is a misconception. The key word is "perceived.")
- And finally, which side do you personally agree with more and why? (Refer to your personal experiences, here. If you have dealt with this issue in your personal life, work, teaching, etc., include that information in your answer.)
- Make sure to include in-text citations (when appropriate) from supporting articles that you found.

Section III

Inclusion and the Least Restrictive Environment

Chapter 6

Least Restrictive Environment
How Does LRE Impact Learning for General Education Students?

Ashlea Rineer-Hershey

PICTURE THIS: You are with a group of fellow parents at a community event. One of the parents mentions that his child is part of a co-taught classroom where there are special education students included in his child's class along with a special education teacher who supports those students. The parent shares that some of the special education students have emotional and behavioral issues. He expresses his concern that his child may not be learning as much or at the level he should be due to these other students. The parents all begin to chime in on their thoughts about whether this is appropriate for the other students. Can needs of all children be met in an inclusive classroom?

What Is the Issue?

Inclusive education or inclusion describes the successful education of students who have special learning needs with the appropriate supports and services to participate and benefit in general classroom settings and other natural environments. Inclusive education implies more than physical proximity between students with and without disabilities. In inclusive schools and classrooms, students with disabilities are valued as contributing members of the school community, leading to a sense of belonging in the classroom and community at large (Rineer-Hershey, 2017).

Throughout the history of special education, a significant progression has occurred regarding the inclusion of special education students in the general education classrooms. For many years, students with any type of special learning needs, including intellectual, behavioral, and physical disabilities, were segregated into separate schools, programs and/or classrooms. Throughout the history of special education, a critical shift has occurred that has allowed students with special needs to benefit from the opportunities available to them in the general education classroom.

In present day, schools are held accountable to including these students with their typical peers as much as possible if it meets their individual learning needs. In schools across the nation, nearly 62.2% of students are included for at least 80% or more of their school day in the general education classroom (National Center for Education Statistics, 2017).

Inclusive school buildings and classrooms strive to provide all learners equal access to the general education classroom, general education teacher, and general education peers while still giving these students the individualized programming that meets their needs through special education, English as a second language, or other types of support. Additionally, inclusive classrooms allow general education students without a special education diagnosis to receive instruction that addresses their individual strengths, challenges, and diversity (Rineer-Hershey, 2017).

As inclusive practices are increasingly more prevalent in schools across the United States, questions about the impact on students without special needs often arise.

Parents, teachers, and communities often ask questions regarding how the other students in the classroom will be impacted by inclusion. What happens to the instruction in the classroom? Do these students hold back the others from learning at the same pace? Do their behaviors impede the learning of others? This chapter will reflect on the law, research, and academic achievement of all students related to the topic of including students and its impact on general education students.

What Does the Law Say?

We will begin this chapter with a careful review of the key federal law that shapes the reason for inclusion for special education students in general education classrooms. This law is the crux of this chapter. The law makes it clear that all children must be given the opportunity to be included in the general education setting no matter their individual educational needs.

Beginning with the initial enactment of the Individuals with Disabilities Education Act (IDEA) in 1975, a major emphasis was placed on our nation to provide quality education for students with special education needs. The law includes six key areas that clearly call on public school districts to ensure that all children with disabilities are provided with the equal opportunity to fully participate in public school education that meets their individual needs (Bartlett, 1993).

First adopted in 1975 and then amended in 2004, IDEA focuses on six major principles including free appropriate public education (FAPE), appropriate evaluations to determine special education eligibility, individualized education plans (IEP), least restrictive environments (LRE), parent involvement in a child's placement decision, and procedural safeguards to protect a child and parent's rights. Each will be discussed more deeply (Osborne & DiMattia, 1994). Although it took many years for schools to be held accountable to what was mandated in IDEA, in present time special education more closely reflects what was outlined in the federal law.

Six Key Areas

1. Free Appropriate Public Education (FAPE)

Under IDEA, every child who qualifies for special education is entitled to what is called a free, appropriate public education. IDEA stresses special education and other related services that must be designed to meet the individual needs of each child. Additionally, the education provided to each special education child must also support him or her as he or she transitions to adulthood and prepare him or her for appropriate employment and the skills necessary to live independently. Public schools are required to ensure that every child receives FAPE.

2. Appropriate Evaluation

Secondly, IDEA requires that school conduct appropriate evaluations of students who are thought to be exceptional. An evaluation must be conducted by a trained and knowledgeable evaluator using reputable and research-based evaluation materials. They must also be administered free of discrimination of any kind. In addition, the evaluation must be completed in a timely manner and address the specific areas of need for that particular student. The evaluation must provide sound recommendations regarding the child's eligibility for special education and critical recommendations.

3. Individualized Education Plan

The individualized education plan (IEP) was established by the IDEA to ensure each child has access to a free appropriate public education (FAPE). The IEP was defined through IDEA as a written document that is developed by an IEP team with specific required members to be involved in its development including the parent(s)/guardian(s), special education teacher, general education teacher, and local education agency representative (building or district administrator capable of making financial decisions).

Required sections in the IEP include present levels of academic performance, annual goals and objectives, specially designed instruction, transition services when a student reaches age 16, and a section that outlines when a student will not participate in the general education classroom and why.

4. Least Restrictive Environment

IDEA places a strong importance on the decision of the child's educational placement. Specifically, IDEA is very clear that a child's placement must be least restrictive. The term "least restrictive" implies that the child has the most opportunity to benefit from time in the general education classroom with typical peers as well as has an opportunity to learn from general education teachers and be taught through the general education curriculum.

Much litigation has occurred at the state and federal level in regard to LRE. The results of those court cases have been clear. No matter how significant a child's disability, the LRE must always be considered beginning with the general education classroom. If an IEP team determines that a student cannot be satisfactorily educated in a general education setting, then the team must make clear efforts to determine the LRE for that student outside of the general classroom.

5. Parent Involvement

Along with LRE, when making a decision for a child's educational placement, the IDEA is very clear that parents/guardians must be highly involved in the educational placement decision. Under this provision with IDEA, the local education agency (LEA) must ensure that the parents/guardians of any child who qualifies for an IEP must be involved and in agreement with any decision regarding the educational placement and LRE for that child.

IDEA also stipulates that parents must be given notification and accommodations in order to participate in all meetings regarding evaluation or planning. Additionally, parents have an opportunity to call a meeting at any time to discuss concerns and changes that may be needed in the IEP. Parents also always retain the right to refuse evaluation of their child.

6. The Procedural Safeguards

The last principle included in IDEA is the establishment of procedural safeguards to protect students and parents throughout the special education process. The procedural safeguards have two purposes. The first is to protect parental access to educational placement and transition planning. The second is that the safeguards include a clear dispute resolution process. Parents can use this process to resolve disagreements over educational placement or other concerns regarding their child's educational needs with the local education agency (LEA). If disagreements arise, parents have the right to request mediation or due process hearings through a state-level process and can also appeal to go to the state and federal court system.

How Does This Affect Schools?

Each local education agency (LEA) or school district is required to follow the mandates outlined in IDEA. Because of these specific requirements for LEAs, since the enactment of IDEA in 1975, many new trainings, programs, and creative thinking have been required to successfully integrate special education students back into their neighborhood schools and many times into the general education classroom. Slowly but surely these changes can be clearly seen across classrooms in the United States. In present day, you will find students with various significant disabilities, such as autism, intellectual disability, multiple disabilities, and children who are blind and/or deaf who take part in the day-to-day activities and educational opportunities in their local schools.

LEAs have gone to great lengths to evolve their programs to clearly meet the needs of diverse learners in grades K–12. The impact on schools requires much more effort and careful planning to ensure there are programs and supports that adequately meet the diverse academic, social, emotional, and behavioral needs of children with special needs.

Additionally, schools are often forced to hire additional teachers with certifications in special education as well as various therapists and paraprofessional support to adequately meet the requirements of FAPE in the students' LRE.

There are significant positive implications for schools as well. Children with IEPs have a greater opportunity to make progress academically and behaviorally when they are included with their general education peers. This creates increased student achievement in the LEA that reflects positively on that LEA via state standardized assessments. This, of course, increases parent satisfaction with the school district. It can often allow schools to receive increased funding from their state as well.

Parent satisfaction is increased in other ways as well. In inclusive classroom environments, parents often feel much more fulfilled as members of their child's educational setting. They feel they are members of their child's school community just as the parents of typical children do. Families feel much more integrated into their child's school community, which allows them and their child to feel accepted and valued.

LEAs will often save significant amounts of money by keeping their students in their neighborhood schools instead of sending them to tuition-based programs in a separate school entity. There are cost savings from decreased need for out-of-district transportation and tuition and therapy.

There are many benefits for LEAs as they increase inclusive practices to keep more of their students in their own neighborhood schools rather than sending them out to other programs. However, even more important than the benefits to the LEA are the benefits to the students.

What Is the Impact on Students Needing Special Education or 504 Plan Services?

As the pressure to provide inclusive practices for students continues to increase, LEAs are rising to the occasion and finding ways to integrate these students successfully back into their neighborhood schools. The opportunity for these children to attend schools with their typical peers are countless. A few of the most important benefits to discuss are outlined in this section.

There are many positive implications for inclusion for the special education students, and many of those are specific to increased and improved self-concept, peer relationships, and role models from typical peers (Peterson & Hittie, 2004). Research supports the idea that students with special needs have increased opportunities to build beneficial friendships with students without disabilities. These friendships help support children's self-concept and create increased opportunities for social interactions and the building of relationships.

Children have positive peer role models in typical children who demonstrate appropriate grade-level academic, social, and behavioral skills. Even without any significant changes in behavior management for a student, research often shows that by having many role models of appropriate behaviors in the classroom, students quickly begin to demonstrate grade-level behavioral and social skills. This opportunity is not available for students with special needs when they are placed in separate schools that only educate other students with IEPs.

Academically, there are many benefits to students with special needs as well. Research shows that these students show an increased achievement of IEP goals (Peterson & Hittie, 2004). The reason this is evidenced is through the greater access students are given to the general education curriculum as well as the general education teachers who are content areas experts in their area of curriculum expertise. Additionally, students have increased opportunities for enhanced skills acquisition and generalization of those skills through opportunities and experiences in the general education classroom.

One other benefit that is important to note is that IEP teams that work with children in the inclusive setting often have much higher expectations for students. When comparing the inclusive classroom environment to a separate school only designed for similar students with special education needs, there is a significant difference in the expectations set forth for the child. In the inclusive classroom environment, the child with the IEP is challenged more rigorously and given additional opportunities to extend his or her knowledge and abilities. In the separate school setting designed only for special education students, the academic and behavioral expectations are often less rigorous and do not allow students to grow to the same degree.

What Is the Impact on General Education Students?

Now it is time to reflect back to the question in the title of this chapter, "How does least restrictive environment impact learning for general education students?" Many positives have been presented for inclusive practices when reflecting on the LEA, as well as the special education students, but are there any benefits to the general education students? This section will present overall benefits to this group of students but also look specifically at the academic implications for general education students included in the same classroom with students needing diverse educational accommodations and modifications.

In the inclusive classroom setting, all students have opportunities to learn from each other's differences. When we consider general education students, inclusion provides increased opportunities to develop meaningful relationships with peers who have differences. General education students learn to have an increased appreciation and acceptance of individual differences as well as an increased understanding and acceptance of diversity in general. Students learn to respect all people, and these opportunities help to prepare them for life in an inclusive society as an adult.

Academically, there are also increased opportunities to allow general education students to continue to grow and be challenged, even if all their peers are not at the same level intellectually or cognitively. Opportunities to master activities by practicing and teaching others are more frequent in the inclusive classroom. Students who are at a higher level can serve as peer mentors to other students. Through this experience they too gain a better understanding of new skills.

Research does show there are greater academic outcomes for all students in the general education classroom (Peterson & Hittie, 2004; Schwarz, 2006). Because teachers are required to meet the learning needs of all students in their classroom, they are often challenged to provide instruction that is more differentiated to address various learning styles and needs. The diverse approach that is needed to meet the needs of all learners is often much more powerful in educating any student in the classroom, whether he or she is a gifted learner, a learner right on track, or one who is struggling in some area. An inclusive classroom has more resources for all students. The classroom teacher is often much more capable of providing the dynamic instruction needed to meet all student needs. Additionally, an inclusive classroom is much more likely to have a co-teacher or a paraprofessional providing support. This allows for a lower teacher to student ratio and for a second approach to instruction in the classroom, which benefits all students.

Additionally, there was no research identified that showed any negative effects from inclusion, when it is implemented with the necessary supports and accommodations, for students to actively participate in the classroom and in turn make gains toward IEP goals.

Conclusion

Overall, this chapter presented a strong review of the law related to special education and inclusive practices, which was founded in IDEA. IDEA mandates that inclusion in the general education classroom be considered first for every student despite his or her special needs. Only after considering this as a placement option can the IEP team consider more restrictive educational placements. Additionally, many reasons to support the use of inclusive classroom placements were presented that benefit the special education but also the general education students in the classroom. In conclusion, no negative implications were supported in this chapter that showed that general education students would be missing out on educational experiences or opportunities. Instead, the chapter shared countless ways that all students benefit from the inclusive classroom setting.

References

Bartlett, L. D. (1993). Mainstreaming: On the road to clarification. *Education Law Reporter*, 76, 17–25.

Downing, J., & Snell, M. (2008). *Including students with severe and multiple disabilities in typical classrooms: Practical strategies for teachers*. Baltimore, MD: Paul H. Brookes Publishing.

Dubow, S. (1989). Into the turbulent mainstream: A legal perspective on the weight to be given to the least restrictive environment in placement decisions for deaf children. *Journal of Law and Education*, 18(2), 215–228.

Individuals with Disabilities Education Act of 1990, 20 U.S.C. § 1401, et seq.

Individuals with Disabilities Education Act of Regulations, 34 C.F.R. § 300, et seq.

Osborne, A., G. & DiMattia, P. (1994). The IDEA's least restrictive environment mandate: Legal implications.*Exceptional Children*, 61(1), 6–14.

Peterson, M., & Hittie, M. (2004). *Inclusive teaching: Creating effective schools for all learners*. Boston, MA: Allyn & Bacon.

Sesikin, S., Shamblin, A., & Dibley, D. (2002). *Don't laugh at me*. Berkeley, CA: Tricycle Press.

Schwarz, P. (2006). *From disability to possibility: The power of inclusive classrooms*. Portsmouth, NH: Heinemann.

National Center for Education Statistics. (2017). *Digest of education statistics, 2016*.

Villa, R., & Thousand, S. (2005). *Creating an inclusive school*. Alexandria, VA: Association for Supervision and Curriculum.

EXTENSION ACTIVITIES

Discussion Activities

1. What are the benefits of inclusion for parents, special education students, general educations, and general and special education teachers? Identify two benefits for each member of the IEP team.
2. What potential barriers do you see toward creating an inclusive classroom? List and explain two.
3. How do you think co-teaching could be used to further support students in the inclusive classroom? What research can you use to support your response?

Write a Letter Assignment

Pick a side:

1. Write a letter from a general education teacher's point of view to his or her building principal as to why he or she should not have any special education students added to his or her general education English class.

2. Write a letter from a special education teacher's point of view as to why his or her student should be included in the general education classroom even though his or her student has skill deficits in reading as well as has issues with attention and focus.

Discussion Paper

After reading this chapter, find a minimum of two additional articles that support this topic and write a double-spaced discussion paper following APA guidelines, including a bibliography page, to address the following:

- Before reading this chapter, my opinion on this issue was _____.

- In your own words, what is the issue at hand?

- Analyze what you see as the two sides of this issue.

- Identify a perceived misconception from either side. (When doing this, list the actual sentence(s) or portion of the sentence, citing the page number that you are making reference to, then write your response as to why you think it is a misconception. The key word is "perceived.")

- And finally, which side do you personally agree with more and why? (Refer to your personal experiences, here. If you have dealt with this issue in your personal life, work, teaching, etc., include that information in your answer.)

- Make sure to include in-text APA citations (when appropriate) from supporting articles that you found.

Section IV

Diversity

Chapter 7

Special Education and Socioeconomic Status

Is There a Misrepresentation Among Minority Groups?

Rachel N. McCann

PICTURE THIS: You are a district administrator visiting a school as part of your regular observations of buildings in the district. As you walk through the general education classrooms, you notice not only strong instruction but that at least 98% of the students are White. When you visit the self-contained special education classrooms, you notice not only unstructured instruction but that there are no white students in the classes. Each class is made up of African American and Latino students. Your conversations with the teachers give you information about some of the students. The African American student was placed in an emotional behavior disorder classroom because he has a difficult time staying seated. The Hispanic student with hearing aids is placed in a deaf and hard of hearing class where American Sign Language is used. This was determined to be the best setting for him due to him wearing hearing aids and reading below grade level. When you follow up with the school-level administrators, you begin to have a discussion with them not only about the quality of the instruction of the students in the self-contained classes but also why they are made up of minority students. You ask what the special education referral process look like in the building.

What Is the Issue?

Special education services have many benefits for students with disabilities and for years have provided many children with services that have set them up for success in their post-academic life. However, special education can be a huge disservice to students who do not need it.

For decades, reports have stated that public schools in the United States have an issue of overrepresentation of minorities in special education. Between 1989 and 2009, the percentage of minority students such as Hispanic American, African American, Asian American and Native American have increased in U.S. public schools from 32% to 45% (Ford, 2012). Some of these groups are already the majority in some American school districts. However, along with the growth of non-White students came the growth of referrals of minorities into special education, with most of the referrals for African American boys (Ford, 2012). This overrepresentation of students can occur when "the percentage of the percentage of minority students in special education exceeds the percentage of these students in the total population" (Miles, 2016, p. 252).

For special education, the proportion of any group of minorities should reflect the general population. However, minorities are overwhelmingly the largest population of students served under the Individual with Disabilities Education Act (IDEA). For example, African American students make up almost 15% of students in general education but represent more than 20% of students in special education (Miles, 2016).

Researchers long have debated and have researched the causes of this overrepresentation of minorities in special education. Among the causes acknowledged have been race, gender, and socioeconomic status (SES). One of the areas that has been at the forefront in recent years has been SES.

A family's SES has been defined as the income, occupation, and education of those living in the household, and a family's SES status can be high, middle, or low (IRIS Center, 2012). Students from low SES families typically achieve at lower levels than students from higher level SES families. Students from low SES families begin kindergarten with lower language skills than their peers and score on average 10% lower than the national average in academic areas such as math and reading (IRIS Center, 2012). This particular group of children has issues keeping up with their peers because their families often do not have the time, funds, or adequate education to advocate for a better educational outcome for their children (Valverde, 2013). "High-risk environments, such as living in poverty, shift the entire curve of achievement to the left, so that there is an increase in the number of children with special needs at the lower end and a decrease in the number of high achievers who may be identified as gifted at the upper end" (National Research Council, 2002, p. 97).

As early as 1968, scholars started to comment on the overrepresentation of students from marginalized cultural and economic backgrounds in special education classes (Dunn, 1968). Harry and Anderson (1994) indicated in a study that the primary recipients of special education services in its beginning were students of color and those of low socioeconomic status. Since then, researchers have examined the factors that have contributed to the disproportionate number of non-White students in special education programming.

Research by the Southern Education Foundation found that nearly 51% of students in U.S. public schools are considered low income (Motoko, 2015). A recent study from Portland State University stated that because African American and Hispanic students often come from lower SES families compared to White students, many may not achieve as high as the White students in academic areas (Shifrer, 2018). This leads to these students being referred to special education (Shifrer, 2018; Valverde, 2013). An average of seven million children receive special education services from the Individuals with Disabilities Education Act; however, four and a half million of these children live in homes with incomes of $50,000 or less (Koseki, 2017).

Additionally, children of low socioeconomic status who receive special education services may be in either a school district or school that already has issues serving students from low-income families (Valverde, 2013). Schools with a high level of socioeconomically challenged students often are unable to hire stronger veteran certified teachers; these schools typically hire educators with weaker qualifications such as years of experience and certification (Presley, White, & Gong, 2005). Furthermore, schools in these low SES communities do not have as many resources as districts with a higher SES population; these schools often have fewer staff members, increasing extra tasks on special education teachers already swamped by paperwork and planning instruction for their students (Phillips, 2008). A Yale study found that general education teachers spend an average of 1.6 hours per week on paperwork compared to special education teachers who take an average of 4.7 hours a week to complete their paperwork (Phillips, 2008).

However, there are those who disagree that socioeconomics is a factor into whether a child is referred into special education. In 2006, O'Connor and DeLuca Fernandez posited that it is not poverty but schools who determine who is disabled, thus leading to disproportionality. The researchers noted that White students are the "norm" to which all students must adhere (O'Connor & DeLuca Fernandez, 2006). Furthermore, they discussed a 2002 National Research Council (NRC) paper that noted that it is the early interactions between parents and children that dictates how successful a child will be in school no matter their socioeconomic background. The 2002 report stated that the "weight of successful development in the early years falls most heavily on the child's relationships with primary adult caregivers," stating that verbal interactions and discipline practices are also key in predicting future academic success since research over the years has shown that these students start kindergarten with smaller vocabularies and high physical aggression (NRC, 2002, p. 121).

What Does the Law Say?

In 1954, the landmark *Brown vs. Board of Education* of Topeka case ruled that separate schools for White and Black students was unconstitutional. However, in the 1966 congressionally authorized Equality of Educational Opportunity report, also known as the Coleman Report, its author suggested that socioeconomic integration of schools could increase achievement better than any other strategy that schools could implement (Wells, Fox, & Cordova-Cobo, 2016). However, the issue of the integrating students of different socioeconomic statuses is still a problem as a large number of socioeconomically challenged minority children are being placed into in special education programs. Since first being recognized in literature by Dunn (1968) 50 years ago, the topic has been put under the microscope in literature and in federal policies, such as the 2004 IDEA amendments, that require state monitoring of disproportionality and case law (see *Guadalupe Organization v. Tempe Elementary School District No. 3*, 1978 and *Larry P. v. Riles*, 1984) (Sullivan & Bal, 2013).

Recognizing students from a low socioeconomic background came to the forefront during the 2000 presidential campaign between George W. Bush and Al Gore as both candidates promised to close the achievement gap between both economically disadvantaged and non-economically disadvantaged students (Barton, 2003). After Bush became the nation's leader in January 2001, both Democrats and Republicans supported the No Child Left Behind Act (NCLB). The act held schools accountable for all students, including those from low socioeconomic backgrounds, as all students were to be at a proficient performance level in all academic subject areas by 2014 (Barton, 2003). If any group of students, including those receiving special education services, failed to progress, an entire school would be considered a failing institution.

As the nation's 44th president, Barack Obama, near the end of his second term of president, and his administration issued a policy called the "Equity in IDEA" Act that required states to monitor how their school districts would identify and serve students with disabilities who were minorities (Samuels & Harwin, 2018). The idea was for all states to determine if school districts were identifying and ultimately "punishing" minority students in special education at a higher rate than their neighboring school districts, which became known as "significant disproportionality" (Samuels & Harwin, 2018; Strauss, 2018). Significant disproportionality also examined when school districts identified, placed students in more restrictive settings, or disciplined minority students at a higher rate than their White peers (Strauss, 2018). Previously. as part of the reauthorization of IDEA in 1997, each state was tasked with monitoring these issues but could decide how they would examine the disproportionality (Samuels & Harwin, 2018).

Currently, states are continuing to tackle the issue to reduce minorities in special education (Samuels & Harwin, 2018). Disproportionality has been described as a "paradox of special education" allowing educators to identify and allocate needed services and any additional resources for students with disabilities (Donovan & Cross, 2002, p. 20). However, placement into special education can lead to stigmatization, segregation, low expectations from teachers, and weak curriculum (Donovan & Cross, 2002). Furthermore, placing a student into special education who doesn't need to be there is a denial of a free and appropriate public education due to placing a student in a restrictive environment.

How Does This Affect Schools?

Researchers have stated that the greatest predictor of educational and social failure in the United States is poverty (Jordan, 2005; Togut, 2012). A National Research Council panel on high-risk youth report found that 40% of Black youth live in long-term poverty situations and live in "economically depressed neighborhoods" with high crime (Jordan, 2005; Togut, 2012). Children who go to school in these areas often have teachers who have low expectations for their academic performance (Jordan, 2005; Togut, 2012). Because these schools are most often low performing and have weak academic standards, the low-income Black students are grouped into low-ability or average courses. These students do not receive enough support in the classroom and are then recommended to receive special education. This is in contrast to higher income schools found in White communities that provide options for average, above average, and honor classes for students; these schools typically do not have as many special education students (Togut, 2012).

It should be noted that a President's Commission on Excellence in Special Education found that teacher referrals make up 80% of students who are placed into special education (Department of Education, 2001; Jordan, 2005). Other studies have shown that teacher judgment is the biggest factor in identifying students who need to be placed into special education classes (Frato, Hostutler, Kunesh, Noltemeyer, & Sarr-Kerman, 2012; Jordan, 2005). These students are often placed because of teachers' beliefs that the children are not motivated, have little intellectual ability, and have an "inadequate home environment"; in these cases there has been no consideration into the environment in the classroom and how they are helping their learning experiences (Jordan, 2005).

What Is the Impact on Students Needing Special Education?

A recent study from Portland State University stated that because minority students such as African American and Hispanic children often are at a socioeconomic disadvantage compared to their White peers they may not perform as well as these students, thus leading to a learning disabled diagnosis (Lardieri, 2018). Research has found that children from low SES families develop their academic skills slower than their peers from higher SES families (Morgan, Farkas, Hillemeier, & Maczuga, 2009). The American Psychological Association found that children from low SES families often have poor cognitive development, memory, and socioemotional processing (American Psychological Association, n.d.).

Because many of these minority students from low SES families are struggling in their general education classrooms, they are being found eligible for special education classes despite not having an actual disability (Rebora, 2011). Because these students are receiving labels that do not suit them, they receive the wrong education and are placed in a restrictive environment (Gentry, 2009). Having a special education label can affect a student's self-esteem; for those who were mislabeled, they feel they have some sort of disability, which can have a negative impact on them emotionally (Gentry, 2009). Furthermore, students in special education have a high rate of dropping out of high school and limited opportunities for their future due to not receiving a quality education.

In a 2015 article, Ford and Toldson said that research over several decades has examined the U.S. school population and has indicated that special education programs have been utilized to separate "unwanted students" from the general education population. African American and Hispanic students who are typically male are most often the most susceptible to institutional bias, thus leading to their overidentification into special education programs. Studies have shown that minority students are 2.3 times more likely to be labeled with a mild intellectual disability when compared to a White student (Gentry, 2009). One of the largest special education programs that African American students are put into is emotional and behavior disorder (EBD) programming (Chinn & Hughes, 1987; Gage, 2013). One of the precursors for EBD referrals is low academic performance and excessive exclusionary discipline actions, and African American students nationally have the highest rates of discipline and suspensions, even over general education students (Cartledge & Robinson-Ervin, 2016).

An additional group of students who have been affected are English language learners. A 2005 study by Salzman found that the population of children in U.S. schools had increased by almost 12% and that students who were English language learners had dramatically increased by 54 percent. Students who are Hispanic were 60% of the English language learners, which was the largest group (Salzman, 2005).

Another group of researchers learned about a majority of teachers at one school that often quickly took English language learners who were Hispanic to an instructional support team because the teachers believed that the academically struggling students had a learning disability (Sanchez, Parker, Akbayin, & McTigue, 2010). The teachers were unaware of effective, research-based strategies to assist the English language learners in the general education setting (Sanchez, Parker, Akbayin, & McTigue, 2010). Instead of providing effective strategies, the students were placed into special education despite not having an actual disability. Salzman (2005) noted that minority children are receiving special education labels such as "emotionally disabled" and "intellectually disabled" because of teachers misinterpreting behavior issues and cultural differences. While some parents are fully aware of their rights in special education, many low SES families do not have the time nor the resources to advocate for their child's rights (Butrymowicz & Mader, 2018).

Parents who do know better often don't want to deal with months or years of court battles or may not have the time or resources to fight with schools. Many parents said that advocating for their children's rights can feel like a full-time job. Even when students get the services to which they're entitled, some parents said that schools and teachers don't grasp how individual disabilities affect different children differently or have reasonable expectations for what their children should be able to do.

What Is the Impact on Students in General Education?

As many school districts focus on improving instruction in their classrooms to help improve graduation rates across the country, for some teachers the mind shift of increasing expectations for students can prove to be a challenge. At many low SES schools, teachers have been found through various studies of having lower expectations of students, which does more harm than good (Butrymowicz & Mader, 2018). Students served in general education at these low SES schools, often under the care of an inexperienced teacher, are not being instructed properly. As previously mentioned, schools in these low SES communities do not have as many resources as districts with a higher SES population (Phillips, 2008). These schools may have outdated textbooks and technology compared to schools with a higher SES population. Without the extra supports such as newer textbooks and computers to access Internet resources that might not be available at home, these students fall further behind. While many students from low socioeconomic families may be referred and placed into special education because they are not receiving quality education from teachers, students who are not being referred for special education also suffer from the lack of quality education (Butrymowicz & Mader, 2018).

Another impact on students in general education is not experiencing students who are different from them. As the United States continues to become more diverse, it is important that everyone from administrators to children understand cultural differences between us all. Experts and parents agree that students who do have actual learning disabilities perform better academically and socially in the same classroom as their peers in general education (Butrymowicz & Mader, 2018). One group of researchers noted that when students are exposed to students who are different from them, either by race or socioeconomic status, these children are able to share different perspectives and ideas that lead to improving cognitive skills such as critical thinking (Wells, Fox, Cordova-Cobo, 2016).

Other studies have found that some students in general education at low SES schools are unfairly targeted. Some students have been treated differently during the initial stages of being tested for special education eligibility based on their race (Skiba et al., 2001). In Gottlieb, Gottlieb, and Trongone's 1991 study, they discovered that minority children who were referred for special education evaluations were selected randomly by teachers and that some of the children were referred for only behavioral issues. While the regular classroom may not be the best learning environment for all students, it is highly desirable for all who can benefit. It provides contact with same age peers and prepares all students for the diversity of the world beyond the classroom. However, schools need to provide the appropriate help to students, whether they are of low SES status or not.

Not only are students in general education impacted but teachers as well. Many general education teachers have not had opportunities to receive proper training in special education or how to improve the reading or math skills of students who may be academically behind (Butrymowicz & Mader, 2018). Despite the fact that all students in a general education classroom walk in with varied skill sets, teachers are not prepared with how to deal with students who may have behavior challenges or who may speak a different language at home.

Conclusion

Whether or not socioeconomic status is a leading factor into the disproportionate number of minorities served in special education, the issue remains that this population of students is academically lagging behind their peers. Even though IDEA aims to provide students who truly need special education access to an education that will teach them to be independent and to be able to be employed after they graduate school, these goals are not being met in low SES communities. Many low SES parents are unaware of due process in special education and do not have money to hire an expert or advocate to help them navigate public education. The students of these parents will continue to struggle in programs that they may not need to be in.

So, how is this issue solved? One school district in the Metro Atlanta area is strengthening its early intervention supports for low-income families in order to give students from low SES backgrounds a chance to receive research-based interventions from district staff before they even begin pre-K. Many other school districts are providing supports for families such as reading awareness by offering free books to families with low incomes to promote reading.

Because of overrepresentation, many researchers feel that the overrepresentation of minority students in special education programs needs to be addressed. Some feel that those who work in schools should examine their assumptions about students who have different backgrounds from their own to be able to understand students' cultural and learning differences (Jordan, 2005; Togut, 2012). Many researchers and groups have suggested ways to help alleviate the issue and cut back on the number of young African Americans in the special education classroom.

A researcher has suggested that teachers of all races become more "culturally responsive" by receiving training to learn how to end prejudices and to learn how to work with different cultures in the classroom to reduce overrepresentation (Ford, 2012; Hoover, 2012). Training should also include working with assessment practices to help with early prevention tactics to prevent a child from ending up in special education classes as well as intervention processes (Togut, 2012). This training will also include how to tell whether a child is in need of an individualized education plan or a different type of instruction that he or she can understand (Togut, 2012). This can also include teachers using culturally responsive interventions, materials, and procedures in the classroom (Hoover, 2012). Culturally responsive teaching is a pedagogy that highlights the importance of including all of a school's cultural references within its learning and school environment by focusing on student backgrounds, interests, and experiences (Ladson-Billings, 1994). Another suggestion is for teachers to learn improved behavior management practices that will work with all students. This will address class school discipline and classroom disruption issues that have plagued teachers in the past (Milner & Tenore, 2010).

An additional proposed strategy is to change the makeup of the school through hiring practices. Those who can understand Black students the most are Black teachers themselves. By hiring a more diverse staff, teachers can support each other in learning about one another's differences as well as give children more Black role models (Togut, 2012).

Another solution to cut back on disproportionality is to change the way that students are being taught. Research has proposed that teachers can help students make connections between what they are learning in class and their own experiences so that they can make knowledge and content more relevant (Jordan, 2005; Togut, 2012). Children who are in homes where education may not be as valued will become more interested in what is being taught in class if it relates to their community and will be more apt to pay attention. For example, one math teacher used basketball to teach probability in math to a group of minority students in special education as this was a shared interest among the children. All the students were engaged in the lesson as it pertained to a subject (basketball) they all enjoyed. This allows teachers and students to extend their knowledge beyond the classroom so that what children learn is more relevant to them and their communities (Togut, 2012).

One of the largest initiatives that many schools across the United States are adopting is response to intervention, commonly known by the acronym RTI. The RTI model is a method of providing at-risk students intense instruction at their current academic level to improve their skills in order to prevent a referral to special education (Barnes & Harlacher, 2008). This method is currently being used as a preventative measure by many schools to address reading difficulties and identify students who appear to be at risk for academic failure; this is to ensure that students receive adequate instruction before they start to show any deficits in academic content areas (Barnes & Harlacher, 2008). Because of the usage of frequent assessment and data-driven decisions that help teachers base their instructional strategies, many students are benefiting from this intervention method (Barnes & Harlacher, 2008). With this early intervention model, special education might be prevented altogether for many Black students across the United States (Feldman, 2011).

There does not seem to be an easy solution to address exact reasons why so many Black students are being referred to special education. There is no quick solution to end poverty in the Black community or end cultural misunderstandings between Black children and White educators. The current response-to-intervention model is showing some promise as a solution to the issue, as it is allowing teachers to tackle any problems with students and examine data that can help guide instruction in the classroom. Because public schools continue to aim for a reduction in the referrals of minority students to special education services, it is hoped that educators across the United States examine ways to reach all students in the classroom no matter their color.

References

American Psychological Association. (n.d.) *Education and socioeconomic status*. Retrieved from https://www.apa.org/pi/ses/resources/publications/education.aspx

Barnes, A. C. & Harlacher, J. E. (2008). Clearing the confusion: Response-to-intervention as a set of principles. *Education & Treatment of Children, 31*(3), 417–431.

Barton, P. E. (2003). *Parsing the achievement gap*. Princeton, NJ: Policy Information Center Educational Testing Service.

Butrymowicz, S., & Mader, J. (2018). The U.S. education system is failing special needs students. *Education Digest, 83*(8), 26–35.

Cartledge, G., & Robinson-Ervin, P. (2016). Issues and interventions for African American students with and at-risk for emotional and behavioral disorders: An introduction to the special issue. *Behavioral Disorders, 41*(4), 175–177.

Chinn, P. C., & Hughes, S. (1987). Representation of minority students in special classes. *Remedial and Special Education, 8*(4), 41–46.

Donovan, M. S., & Cross, C. T. (Eds.). (2002). *Minority students in special and gifted education*. Washington, DC: National Academies.

Dunn, L. M. (1968). Special education for the mildly mentally retarded: Is much of it justifiable? *Exceptional Children, 35*(1), 5–22.

Feldman, J. (2011). Racial perspectives on eligibility for special education: For students of color who are struggling, is special education a potential evil or a potential good? *The American University Journal of Gender, Social Policy & the Law, 20*(1), 183–200.

Ford, D. (2012). Culturally different students in special education: Looking backward to move forward. *Exceptional Children, 78*(4), 391–405.

Ford, D. Y., & Toldson, I. A. (2015, July 5). Study on Black, Hispanic children in special ed wrong, regressive. Retrieved from http://diverseeducation.com/article/76088/

Frato, P., Hostutler, C., Kunesh, C., Noltemeyer, A., & Sarr-Kerman, B. (2012). The effects of teacher characteristics on teacher impressions of and responses to student behaviors. *International Education Studies, 5*(4), 96–111.

Gage, N. A. (2013). Characteristics of students with emotional disturbance manifesting internalizing behaviors: A latent class analysis. *Education and Treatment of Children, 36*(4), 127–145.

Gentry, R. (2009). Disproportionate representation of minorities in special education: How bad? Jane H. LeBlanc Conference in Communication Disorders, State University, Jonesboro, AR.

Gottlieb, J., Gottlieb, B. W., & Trongone, S. (1991). Parent and teacher referrals for a psychoeducational evaluation. *The Journal of Special Education, 25*(2), 155–167.

Harry, B., & Anderson, M. G. (1994). The disproportionate placement of African American males in special education programs: A critique of the process. *Journal of Negro Education, 63*(4), 602–619.

Hoover, J. J. (2012). Reducing unnecessary referrals. *Teaching Exceptional Children, 44*(4), 39–47.

IRIS Center. (2012). *Classroom diversity: An introduction to student differences.* Retrieved from https://iris.peabody.vanderbilt.edu/module/div/

Jordan, K. (2005). Discourses of difference and the overpopulation of Black students in special education. *Journal of African American History, 90*(1), 128–149.

Sanchez, M. T., Parker, C., Akbayin, B., & McTigue, A. (2010). *Processes and challenges in identifying learning disabilities among students who are English language learners in New York State districts.* Washington, DC: Regional Educational Laboratory Northeast and Islands.

Koseki, M. (2017). Meeting the needs of all students: Amending the idea to support special education students from low-income households. *Fordham Urban Law Journal, 44*(3), 793–831.

Ladson-Billings, G. (1994). *The dreamkeepers: Successful teachers of African American children.* San Francisco, CA: Jossey-Bass.

Lardieri, A. (2018, August 21). Study: Minorities labeled learning disabled because of social inequalities. *U.S. News.* Retrieved from https://www.usnews.com/news/education-news/articles/2018-08-21/study-minorities-labeled-learning-disabled-because-of-social-inequalities

Miles, A. (2016). Overrepresentation in special education: Does the idea violate the equal protection clause? *Rutgers Race and the Law Review, 17*(2), 245–265.

Milner, H., & Tenore, F. (2010). Classroom management in diverse classrooms. *Urban Education, 45*(5), 560–603.

Morgan, P. L., Farkas, G., Hillemeier, M. M., & Maczuga, S. (2009). Risk factors for learning-related behavior problems at 24 months of age: Population-based estimates. *Journal of Abnormal Child Psychology, 37*(3), 401–413.

Motoko, R. (2015, January 16). Percentage of poor students in public schools rises. New York Times.

National Research Council. (2002). *Minority students in special and gifted education.* Washington, DC: National Academy Press.

O'Connor, C., & Deluca Fernandez, S. (2006). Race, class, and disproportionality: Reevaluating the relationship between poverty and special education placement. *Educational Researcher, 35*(6), 6–11.

Phillips, E. (2008). When parents aren't enough: External advocacy in special education. *Yale Law Journal, 117*(8), 1802–1853.

Presley, J., White, B., & Gong, Y. (2005). Examining the distribution and impact of teacher quality in Illinois. Policy research report: IERC 2005–2. *Illinois Education Research Council.* Retrieved from https://files.eric.ed.gov/fulltext/ED493170.pdf

Rebora, A. (2011). Keeping special ed in proportion. *Education Week.* Retrieved from https://www.edweek.org/tsb/articles/2011/10/13/01disproportion.h05.html

Salzman, A. (2005, November 20). Special education and minorities. *New York Times.* Retrieved from https://www.nytimes.com/2005/11/20/nyregion/nyregionspecial2/special-education-and-minorities.html

Samuels, C., & Harwin, A. (2018, January 24). Racial disparities in special ed: How widespread is the problem? *Education Week.* Retrieved from https://www.edweek.org/ew/articles/2018/01/24/racial-disparities-in-special-ed-how-widespread.html

Shifrer, D. (2018). Clarifying the social roots of the disproportionate classification of racial minorities and males with learning disabilities. *The Sociological Quarterly, 59*(3), 384–406.

Skiba, R., Horner, R., Chung, C., Rausch, M., May, S., & Tobin, T. (2011). Race is not neutral: A national investigation of African American and Latino disproportionality in school discipline. *School Psychology Review, 40*(1), 85–107.

Strauss, V. (2018, May 4). Are too many minority students identified as disabled? Or are some who need services overlooked? *Washington Post.* Retrieved from https://www.washingtonpost.com/news/answer-sheet/wp/2018/05/04/are-too-many-minority-students-identified-as-disabled-or-are-some-who-need-services-overlooked/?noredirect=on&utm_term=.55855a224767

Sullivan, A., & Bal, A. (2013). Disproportionality in special education: Effects of individual and school variables on disability risk. *Exceptional Children, 79*(4), 475–494.

Togut, T. (2012). The gestalt of the school-to-prison pipeline: The duality of overrepresentation of minorities in special education and racial disparity in school discipline of minorities. *American University Journal of Gender, Social Policy and the Law, 20*(1), 163–181.

U. S. Department of Education. (2001). Twenty-third annual report to Congress on the implementation of the Individuals with Disabilities Act. Washington, DC. Retrieved from https://www2.ed.gov/about/offices/list/osers/osep/index.html?src=mr

Wells, A., Fox, L., & Cordova-Cobo, D. (2016). How racially diverse schools and classrooms can benefit all students. *Education Digest, 82*(1), 17–24.

Valverde, J. R. (2013). A poor idea: Statute of limitations decisions cement second-class remedial scheme for low-income children with disabilities in the third circuit. *Fordham Urban Law Journal, 41*(2), 599–1759.

EXTENSION ACTIVITIES

Discussion Questions

1. Research has stated that culturally responsive teaching can have a positive effect on learning in classrooms. As a school administrator, how would you implement culturally responsive teaching in your building? How will you determine if it is effective?
    a. If there is an issue of a disproportionate amount of minority students of low SES background being placed into special education programs, discuss how you would solve this problem if you were a school administrator.
    b. Identify what laws you are abiding by or that are supporting your decisions.
2. How does a school determine whether a minority student of low SES background truly needs special education services?
    a. Explain how you would determine this if you were the one making the decision.

Write a Letter Assignment

Pick a side:

1. Write a letter from a low SES parent-advocate's view to your child's school administrator outlining the reasons why your child should receive more support in the general education classroom before potentially being considered for special education services.
2. Write a letter from a special education teacher's view opposing having a low SES student of Hispanic origin being placed in your special education classroom.

Discussion Paper

1. After reading this chapter, find a minimum of two additional articles that support this topic and write a double-spaced discussion paper following APA guidelines, including a bibliography page, to address the following:
    a. Before reading this chapter, my opinion on this issue was _____.
    b. In your own words, what is the issue at hand?
    c. Analyze what you see as the two sides of this issue.
    d. Identify a perceived misconception from either side. (When doing this, list the actual sentence(s) or portion of the sentence, citing the page number that you are making reference to, then write your response as to why you think it is a misconception. The key word is "perceived.")
    e. And finally, which side do you personally agree with more and why? (Refer to your personal experiences, here. If you have dealt with this issue in your personal life, work, teaching, etc., include that information in your answer.)
    f. Make sure to include in-text citations (when appropriate) from the supporting articles that you found.

Chapter 8

English Language Learners
Is There an Overidentification of English Language
Learners in Special Education?

Ashlea Rineer-Hershey

PICTURE THIS: You are a first-generation immigrant to the United States from Russia. Your oldest child, a kindergartener, is starting school this year. Your family still speaks Russian often, but you have learned to speak English for your job. However, at home, you and your family speak your first language. As a result, your 5-year old daughter knows very little English. You take her to kindergarten registration. Some staff is there to help you with registration, and they immediately recognize the language barrier for your daughter. They request you give permission to evaluate for special education. You don't understand what this means, but you agree. You want your daughter to have every chance to be successful in school.

What Is the Issue?

Our country was developed and has grown thanks to the immigration of individuals from all over the world. For this reason, the United States has become a melting pot for various cultures, many of those cultures bringing their own religions, values, languages, and educational experiences. As the educational system in the United States has evolved to better meet the needs of students, it has become apparent that in this country we need to be doing something different to meet the needs of our English language learners (ELLs).

ELLs are students between the ages of 3 and 21, enrolled in school, and have a primary or first language other than English. In order to meet their needs, ELLs require specific language instruction, in addition to taking part in grade-level instruction in the other content areas. ELLs are considered the fastest growing population of students in the United States school system. And, according to the National Clearinghouse for English Language Acquisition (NCELA), it is predicted by 2025 that 25% of the student population across the nation will be an ELL (NCELA, 2018).

In recent years, additional policies have been put into the place to protect ELLs and be sure they are receiving appropriate education to support them as they learn the English language while simultaneously participating in their public school education. Recent research has shown that these students are frequently identified as ELLs as well as special education students in need of an IEP.

At dramatic rates, ELLs are being serviced through an IEP. As a result, concerns have arisen regarding the unprecedented rates of ELLs that are also receiving special education services.

Are ELLs being evaluated for special education properly? Are they qualifying for special education simply because of a language barrier? Can the same instructional strategies to educate students with special needs be used to meet the needs of ELLs? These questions and others will be addressed throughout this chapter as well as a reflection on whether there is an overrepresentation of ELLs in special education.

What Does the Law Say?

In the United States, the overrepresentation of children with diverse cultural and linguistic backgrounds and their educational experiences are considered a significant issue faced by the public school system over the past 30 years (Donovan & Cross, 2002). During the 1980s and 1990s, existence of disproportionality in special education began to be treated through federal policy as a type of potential discrimination against English language learners. The Office of Civil Rights (OCR) conducts regular monitoring at the state and local level to address evidence that this may be occurring.

Specifically, federal legislation has been amended to address the diverse needs of ELLs. The Individuals with Disabilities Education Act (IDEA) entitles all individuals with disabilities to a free appropriate public education (FAPE) and mandates nondiscriminatory assessment, identification, and placement of children with disabilities (Donovan & Cross, 2002). The legislation is very clear regarding ELLs. Children are not to be identified as in need of special education because of poor achievement due to environmental disadvantage or ethnic, linguistic, or racial difference.

This is made clear by the prescribed evaluation procedures and the definitions of disability conditions in IDEA. However, nationally, some ethnic groups continue to be overrepresented as disabled, particularly as learning disabled, mildly intellectually disabled, or emotionally disturbed. One research study showed that English language learners were 27% more likely to be placed in special education programs in elementary grades and almost twice as likely to be placed in secondary grades (Artiles, Rueda, Salazar, & Higareda, 2005). State and local representation rates vary widely but in many cases show even clearer patterns of overrepresentation (Oswald & Coutinho, 2001).

The Individuals With Disabilities Education Act (IDEA)

One of the key federal laws that looks to protect the rights of ELLs is IDEA. When IDEA was amended in 1991 and 1997, federal concern became apparent regarding the educational experience of students in special education with a linguistically or culturally diverse background. The 1991 and 1997 amendments to IDEA included a compelling argument that we, as a nation, need to do better when serving students of these diverse backgrounds. Three key areas were addressed within those most recent amendments.

1. The rate of culturally and linguistically diverse children served through special education is much higher than what would be expected based on the actual population of culturally and linguistically diverse students in the general population.
2. Improved efforts are needed to prevent mislabeling students as special education when they are in fact simply struggling academically because of the language and cultural differences.
3. Methods to decrease dropout rates among our students that come from culturally and linguistically diverse backgrounds must be implemented in a systematic process.

As these amendments were put into place, states began to implement their own procedures for public school entities related to the appropriate identification of English language learners in need of special education services. Although the identification processes at the state levels have helped to address the issue, there is still a long way to go. Research shows that ELL students are still being overrepresented in special education (Artiles, Rueda, Salazar, & Higareda, 2005). In additional research, Artiles, Rueda, Salazar, and Higareda (2005) found that students less fluent in their first language and in English were more likely to be overrepresented in special education. More overrepresentation of ELLs receiving special education services was also documented in districts with greater numbers of ELLs.

In addition, there is a growing concern from policymakers that our ELLs are more frequently being educated in restrictive educational settings and that those settings are not always justified based on children's true learning needs. It is critical that advances continue to be sure only ELLs who also have a true special education need are being educated in a more restrictive classroom placement if needed.

How Does This Affect Schools?

As public school entities across the United States continue to evolve toward providing more equal educational opportunities to students across the spectrum of varying needs, it becomes increasingly demanding on educators and administrators to meet the needs of all. The implications of this disproportionality among ELLs require schools to develop more effective policies, procedures, and educational programming. Some key factors must be addressed by schools in order to be sure ELLs are being properly identified and that their educational needs are met.

1. In order to meet the diverse needs, administrators must develop procedures to increase the appropriateness of assessment practices, which lead to the same decisions at the referral, assessment, and placement steps regardless of the race or ethnicity of the student given the same behaviors or symptoms.

2. Administrators must also be sure there is high quality and effective instructional practices in place to benefit all students. If this is in place, we should see improvements in the educational outcomes for all students.

3. In order to receive adequate instruction that allows ELLs to grow, learn, and achieve peak performance, schools must have educators who have skills, expertise, and certification to teach the ELL population of students. These students require a different set of instructional strategies than what might be needed by the typical learner.

4. A change in mind-set must also occur within the school faculty. Administrators must lead their staff as they increase their understanding about the need for differing instructional approaches for ELLs as well as the difference between an ELL and a student in need of an IEP.

As schools work to address the disproportionality that may be evident in their district, it is important for these suggestions to be recognized as critical. Most importantly, the fourth factor can often be the primary area of growth needed to begin to make a significant improvement in the equitable education of ELL students. Daniels (1998) has clearly stated that the disproportionate representation is a significant problem, in and of itself indicative of inherent inequities within our educational system that prejudice outcomes for culturally and linguistically diverse students. Our priority must be to first eliminate the inherent bias that is occurring as these students begin their educational experience in U.S. schools.

Schools must continue to make every effort to monitor disproportionality and develop a plan for reform in their educational practices to better meet the needs of all students. As the needs of ELLs are more clearly identified, schools must create better systems of developed educational plans and programs to meet their unique needs.

What is the Impact on English Language Learners and Students Needing Special Services?

If school districts and entities are properly following the guidelines of IDEA, unique and individual programming will be sought after to address their needs. Schools that adhere to IDEA in terms of ELL students may resemble those serving special education students; however, it should not be assumed the same strategies and instructional techniques will work for both groups. Some of the research-based strategies recommended for ELLs will be shared in this section. They do support diverse learners of all types, as they are educated in the general education classroom.

1. Scaffolding: This consists of providing ELLs with strategic types of supports that help to scaffold the content to a place that is at their level. Scaffolding may consist of using graphic organizers, visual aids, and peer mentoring/supports as some options. As the ELL student's skills develop, some of the scaffolding is pulled away. In turn the ELLs can be given the opportunity and needed support to participate in the general education classroom with the regular curriculum so they can meet rigorous academic standards (Greene, 2013).

2. Flexible grouping: Research suggests that utilizing heterogeneous classrooms is beneficial for ELLs. ELLs need to be given many opportunities to have interactions via group work, partner activities, and so on with peers of different English proficiency levels (Greene, 2013). It is best if ELLs have opportunities for flexible grouping: homogeneously, heterogeneously, or grouped by specific English proficiency skills needs or abilities.

3. Background knowledge: For ELLs to have opportunities to achieve success in the typical grade-level classroom, providing them with relevant background knowledge is critical. The need to have access to the background about a topic that will be the center of the lesson or activate their existing knowledge on a topic is needed to ensure success. This will help increase students' interest and allow them to be more focused on the instructional goals and skills and not learning too much new information at once. Contextual information to ELLs is often critical in their understanding, and their deficits in this area can take away from the focus of learning critical skills needed to move them toward English proficiency (Greene, 2013).

4. Interactive discussion: In order for ELLs to continue to grow their English proficiency and extend their vocabulary, opportunities for extensive discussions with their grade-level peers is paramount (Greene, 2013). Research shares that it is most effective to teach students new vocabulary through extended discussion opportunities after reading or between multiple reading opportunities.

5. Value ELLs linguistic differences: One of the most important ways to support ELLs is to treat their linguistic and cultural differences in the classroom as resources rather than obstacles. Research (Greene, 2013) recommends that classroom teachers reach out to students' families and communities to create learning opportunities in collaboration.

These five strategies are used to support the successful instruction of ELLs in the school setting (Greene, 2013). By utilizing these five recommendations in the classrooms, the needs of ELLs can be met successfully. It will take time for these students to successfully acquire the English language while simultaneously gaining the grade-level skills, but it can happen. These strategies as well as others that embrace the idea of differentiated instruction are imperative in supporting the learning needs of these unique groups of students. Although the process for ELLs to acquire the English language can take up to 7–10 years to meet grade-level norms, it is important to continue to exhibit patience and consistency throughout the process. Similar to special education, these students will often need an individualized approach in their education and in addressing their English proficiency needs.

It should also be noted that through the use of these recommended instructional strategies ELLs remain in the general education classroom with their typical peers. This allows them the opportunity to grow and learn in their cultural and linguistic skills from same-age peers with appropriate English speaking, reading, and writing skills. Although it may be necessary to provide ELLs with small group or individualized instruction for portions of the school day, it is critical for them to also be included in their least restrictive environment through the use of varied instructional strategies.

What Is the Impact on Students in General Education?

For general education students receiving an education alongside ELLs, they should see no change to the quality of their educational programs. Instead they will likely receive a more diverse and individualized educational experience themselves. If the instructional strategies used for ELLs are carried out as research recommends, many teachers will find that these instructional strategies and approaches are often beneficial to other students in the classroom.

Students who may be working below reading benchmark or who have a learning disability often benefit from similar instructional strategies. As the diverse needs in our classrooms continue to change, embracing some of the recommended ELL strategies can only benefit others in the classroom as well. As educators, it is always important to make sure that the needs of all learners are met no matter how diverse they may be, and English language learners are not different. All students have the ability to learn; we just need to find the strategy or method that best meets their needs.

Conclusion

In conclusion, the issue of misrepresentation of ELLs in special education cannot be ignored. As the needs of ELLs become clear, schools are required to develop better educational programs. Federal law mandates that these educational programs are not simply special education services. Instead, they must be unique to the specific learning needs of ELLs. Administrators and educators alike must use research-based instructional strategies to support ELLs in their general education classroom with their typical peers. As research in the area of ELLs continues to grow, our educational programs must evolve to meet those recommendations specific to this population of students. We cannot continue to simply group ELLs with their special education peers in terms of educational programs and instructional techniques. These children can learn and grow in their English proficiency while simultaneously acquiring new grade-level academic, behavioral, and social skills.

References

Artiles, A. J., Rueda, R., Salazar, J. J., & Higareda, I. (2002). English-language learner representation in special education in California urban school districts. In D. J. Losen & G. Orfield (Eds.), *Racial inequity in special education* (pp. 117–136). Cambridge, MA: Harvard Education Press.

Artiles, A. J., Rueda, R., Salazar, J. J., & Higareda, I. (2005). Within-group diversity in minority disproportionate representation: English language learners in urban school districts. *Exceptional Children, 71*(3), 283–300.

Chinn, P. C., & Hughes, S. (1987). Representation of minority students in special classes. *Remedial & Special Education, 8*(4), 41–46.

Daniels, V. I. (1998). Minority students in gifted and special education programs: The case for education equity. *Journal of Special Education, 32*(1), 41–43.

Donovan, M. S., & Cross, C. (Eds.). (2002). *Minority students in special and gifted education*. Washington, DC: National Academy Press.

Garcia, S. & Ortiz, A. (2006). Preventing disproportionate representation: Culturally and Linguistically Responsive Pre-referral Interventions. Teaching Exceptional Children: Practitioner Brief Series, 38(4), 64–68.

Greene, R. (2013). 5 key strategies for ELL instruction. *Teaching Channel*. Retrieved from www.teachingchannel.org.blog/2013/10/25strategies-for-ell-instruction

MacMillan, D. L., & Balow, I. H. (1991). Impact of Larry P. on educational programs and assessment practices in California. *Diagnostique, 17*(1), 57–69.

National Clearinghouse for English Language Acquisition (NCELA). (2018). English language trends for the nation's report card. Bethesda, MD: Author.

Oswald, D. P. & Coutinho, M. J. (2001). Trends in disproportionate representation in special education: Implications for multicultural education. In C. A. Utley & F. E. Obiakor (Eds.), *Special education, multicultural education, and school reform: Components of a quality education for students with mild disabilities* (pp. 53–73). Springfield, IL: Charles C. Thomas.

Parents in Action on Special Education (PASE) v. Joseph P. Hannon. (1980). U.S. District Court, Northern district of Illinois, Easter Division, No. 74 (3586)

Patton, J. M. (1998). The disproportionate representation of African Americans in special education: Looking behind the curtain for understanding and solutions. *Journal of Special Education, 32*(1), 25–31.

Reschly, D. J. (1991). Bias in cognitive assessment: Implications for future litigation and professional practices. *Diagnostique, 17*(1), 86–90.

Reschly, D. J. (1988). Assessment issues, placement litigation, and the future of mild mental retardation classification and programming. *Education and Training in Mental Retardation, 23*(4), 285–301.

Sullivan, A. L. (2011). Disproportionality in special education identification and placement of English language learners. *Exceptional Children, 77*(3), 317–334.

Valenzuela, J. S., Copeland, S. R., Qi, C. H., & Park, M. (2006). Examining educational equity: Revisiting the disproportionate representation of minority students in special education. *Exceptional Children, 72*(4), 425–441.

EXTENSION ACTIVITIES

Discussion Questions

1. Statistically describe the populations of English language learners, special education students, and those that fit both categories in your school district or entity. Do you see any obvious concerns from this data that might lead you to believe there is a misrepresentation occurring in your school's ELL population? Clearly explain this data and why you gave your response to this question.

2. Imagine you are a general education teacher. You have a new ELL student who has registered in your school and will now be a part of your classroom. What will be your first steps to prepare yourself for this new student?

3. What do you feel is the biggest barrier to classroom teachers' ability to meet the needs of ELLs in their general education classroom? Explain your answer.

Develop an ELL Parallel Lesson

Choose a lesson plan that you have written in the past or develop a new one and design and identify modifications for each step in the lesson sequence to address the needs of the ELLs in your classroom. Also, include parallel content materials that will allow the students to work on the same skill areas but using materials at their level.

Discussion Paper

After reading this chapter, find a minimum of two additional articles that support this topic and write a double-spaced discussion paper following APA guidelines, including a bibliography page, to address the following:

- Before reading this chapter, my opinion on this issue was _____.

- In your own words, what is the issue at hand?

- Analyze what you see as the two sides of this issue.

- Identify a perceived misconception from either side. (When doing this, list the actual sentence(s) or portion of the sentence, citing the page number that you are making reference to, then write your response as to why you think it is a misconception. The key word is "perceived.")

- And finally, which side do you personally agree with more and why? (Refer to your personal experiences, here. If you have dealt with this issue in your personal life, work, teaching, etc., include that information in your answer.)

- Make sure to include in-text citations (when appropriate) from supporting articles that you found.

Section V

Related Services and Supplemental Aids and Services (SaS)

Chapter 9

Service and Support Animals
Which Is Most Appropriate in the School Setting?

Toni L. Mild

> **PICTURE THIS:** It's Saturday afternoon and you and some friends decide to go to a local restaurant for lunch. When you get seated, you notice that at the table next to you are a man and woman eating. As you look closer, you also notice that there is a dog with them. You immediately think that it is probably a service animal of some sorts. One of the people that you are with begins questioning why animals are now allowed in restaurants. Your group begins a discussion on the issue—some people supportive of it, some totally against animals being next to them while they eat, shop, etc.

What Is the Issue?

Service animals. Support animals. What is the difference between the two and why are we seeing more and more of them in the many different places that we frequent? There is definitely a difference between the two and there are federal laws in place that protect the rights of people who use one of these types of animals in public settings. Some of the more common animals being used as either service or support are dogs, miniature horses, pigs, parrots, snakes, ferrets, and monkeys. The list of animals being used seems to be growing daily, but there is a difference between support and service animals, and only one of them has provisions set forth by law in terms of overseeing its use.

Support animals are animals that just by their presence make the owner *feel* better. The animals provide a peace and comfort that is not felt without these animals present. There are several types of animals that people use for support. There are currently no laws in place to protect the rights of owners with support animals.

Service animals on the other hand, provide an actual service for their owner. Service animals are most commonly used with individuals who have some sort of handicap or debilitating condition. One of the major differences between a service and support animal is that the service animal has training to assist the owner. The animal provides a service for that individual that he or she is not able to do him- or herself. Tasks that these animals may be responsible for providing could be opening a door for someone with a physical disability, picking up or retrieving a needed item for someone who may require a wheelchair, or sensing that an impending seizure is about to occur for someone who has epilepsy. The tasks that these animals assist their owners with are critical activities that are needed to live their lives on a daily basis. Service animals are not pets but workers. They provide the needed support that the disability prevents their owners from completing.

The most commonly used service animal are dogs. Miniature horses are becoming more common and there is currently a provision in the law that addresses their use, but dogs remain the major provider of service. Some people choose miniature horses due to the cost involved with training and the lifespan of horses over dogs. Miniature horses can live up to 30 years where a dog's average life span is around 10–13 years. The costs associated with breeding and training these service animals can be quite high—upwards of $25,000.00.

What Does the Law Say?

The Americans with Disabilities Act, also known as ADA, has specific portions of the law that talk directly about use of service animals. The two areas of the law that speak directly to service animals are Title II and Title III. Title II of the act addresses state and local government regulations while Title III addresses regulations for public accommodations and commercial facilities. Currently the law only acknowledges dogs as being service animals. And, likely due to this, ADA has set up specific requirements for the use of service dogs. Any Title II or Title III entity must allow a service animal to accompany a person when on his or her property or within his or her place of business.

According to the ADA, "A service animal is a dog that is individually trained to do work or perform tasks for a person with a disability" (U.S. Department of Justice, 2011). Note the two requirements: "individually trained" and "do work/perform a task." For ADA's purposes, the dog must have training and be working or doing a specific duty. The dog must fulfil a specific need that a person with a disability is unable to perform. The ADA addresses that while in a public setting, if the work that the service dog is not immediately known, an employee may ask if the animal is being used to assist them with a disability. They may also ask what service the animal is providing for the person. However, an employee is not allowed to question the type of disability an individual has, ask for proof of the disability, or ask for proof of the type of training the dog has received. Use for a disability and what the work is that is being done are the only two things that can be asked by an employee.

How Does This Affect Schools?

The ADA also states, "Allergies and fear of dogs are not valid reasons for denying access or refusing service to people using service animals" (U.S. Department of Justice, 2011). This has been a common reason used by many entities, including schools, to prohibit the use of service animals. School administrators are seeing an increase in service and support animal requests by parents each year. Determining these requests is not always an easy task for an administrator due to there being many circumstances to take into consideration for each decision.

A student with a disability may require a service dog to assist them in their daily activities as part of their specially designed instruction that is mandated through the Individuals with Disabilities Education Act (IDEA). If there is evidence that a dog would fulfill this student's need for specially designed instruction, the use of this service animal would be written into the student's individualized education plan (IEP), or, if a resident of Pennsylvania, be included in their Chapter 15 Section 504 service plan.

Problems arise, however, when other parents in the district may argue that their son or daughter has severe allergies—so severe that they require their own Chapter 15/504 plan to outline what is to be done when their allergies cause him or her problems in the school day. And yet another set of parents may complain that their child has a very severe fear of dogs due to being brutally bitten in the past. Who wins? Is it the student with the IEP who lists a service dog as a form of specially designed instruction or is it the parents of the students with allergies and a fear of dogs? How does a school district possibly make a sound decision in terms of one child's needs over another's? With all of the responsibilities that districts already have in the education, safety, and support of children, this is one more area that they are having to address on a more frequent basis.

On the other hand, there are also schools that are taking a different approach and incorporating support animals, overseen by faculty members, and using them as a way to bond with students. Some school counselors are using support animals in counseling or therapy sessions for students who are anxious or who have a harder time opening up.

In New York, the Department of Education has partnered with an animal league to provide schools with dogs that have been obedience trained and are better tempered (McKibben 2018). These schools are seeing their student's empathy skills become more developed.

> Lots of times, young people can see in an animal what they can't see in their classmates. And they express a certain kind of empathy, understanding, and compassion that might [be] difficult at other times due to different things going on in their lives. (McKibben, 2018, p. 5).

This approach to using support animals must be well planned and organized by district teams. It may work in some districts but may not be feasible in others. Stakeholders would need to determine whether using support animals in this fashion would benefit their student population.

What Is the Impact on Students Needing Special Education or 504 Plan Services?

Service dogs provide a service just as any other supportive device may. People would rarely question a person's use of a wheelchair, braces, cane, prosthetic, or use of insulin by a person with diabetes, but we often times hear the use of service dogs questioned.

So why is the use of these animals questioned? There are many reasons for this, but two major reasons are caused by (a) a lack of understanding of the need for the use of these animals and (b) the lack of understanding between what a support animal and what a service animal provides its owner. The influx of people bringing emotional support dogs with them everywhere they go has skyrocketed. A support animal functions differently than a service animal does. Emotional support animals usually do not have intense, specific training and provide comfort in regard to their presence, having the ability to reduce anxiety and depression or alleviate loneliness for their owners. One of the major differences between the two is that service dogs provide a specific service to their owners so that they may function as independently as possible in their daily life activities, where a support dog just has to be in the vicinity to assist with their owner's emotional well-being.

As discussed earlier, there may be a benefit in staff having a support animal present in the school for some students with special education and 504 plan needs. Districts would certainly need to determine where the animal would be of benefit and in what classes it is more of a distraction.

What Is the Impact on Students in General Education?

Students with disabilities are in the general education setting on a daily basis. This is mandated through both federal and state laws. The federal law IDEA mandates that school entities look at the "least restrictive environment" (LRE) for students who qualify for special education services. We can go into great discussion as to what the LRE is and is not, but that is an individual determination by the IEP team for each student, so for the purpose of this chapter, we are just going to put LRE in laymen's terms, which can be considered the general education setting: the setting in which students who do not have disabilities are educated. States are obligated to mimic the federal law language in their state regulations. They have the authority to have their own state laws that govern special education and can include additional regulations, but they must follow the minimum mandates established by the federal law. And, if you are a resident of Pennsylvania, the LRE obligations for school districts are greater than in other states. Therefore, students with and without disabilities will be together in the general education setting on a daily basis.

Students without disabilities do not have any special laws that give them additional rights. The only mandates in place to govern them are listed in the state's school code guidelines, within the school district's board policy, or outlined within the student handbook. Therefore, if they have a disagreement or problem with the use of service animals in their classroom, they do not have any rights that would supersede their use.

Teachers as well do not have any rights as to whether they want a service animal in their classroom. As an employee of the school district, they are obligated to follow a student's IEP or 504 plan. The ADA provisions do outline that the owner or handler of the service animal must be able to control it. Therefore, it would not be the teacher's responsibility to keep the dog under control or take care of any of its needs throughout the day.

Having a service dog present in the classroom will require extra work from teachers. They will need to determine how to make something that is currently "not a common fixture," and that the majority of students will be excited about, not take away from the learning environment. It will likely take a while to teach all of the students that the student and the dog will come into contact and to get used to the animal being present. Teachers will have to educate and remind their class frequently about the dog's job and function throughout the school day. With time, education, and a structured classroom, a service animal can definitely be accepted and not be seen as a distraction. Just like anything new that is introduced in the classroom setting, students, teachers, and staff, should be provided with the information and background so that they can understand the need and purpose of the animal. Everyone involved will need time to process this new information and hopefully can then move to the stage of acceptance and ultimately appreciation and respect for service that is being provided.

Some schools are starting to incorporate more and more support animals in the school setting to assist with providing a calming influence, to increase student empathy, and to assist in the overall climate of a school, classroom, or therapy session. This would affect all students in this setting, not just those with IEPs or service plans. One counselor in a West Virginia school uses her therapy dog as an "excuse" for some of the harder-to-reach boys to stop by her office. Telling their friends that they're going to see the dog, rather than going for a therapy session, seems to be more socially acceptable to peers (McKibben, 2018).

Conclusion

In summary, there are two types of animals that people are using these days: support animals and service animals. Support animals fulfill a need of the owner and usually are not formally trained. Service animals, on the other hand, have formal training and are used to complete a function or service that the owner cannot do on his or her own without the animal's assistance. The ADA has provisions in the law that protects the use of service dogs. There are no laws that address or back the use of support animals. There are pros and cons to the use of these animals. Both types of animals have effects on the public sector, including their use in the school setting. Determining the use in the school environment is not an easy task for school employees. Students must always be part of the conversation and that conversation needs to involve all stakeholders.

References

McKibben, S. (2018). Why schools are going to the dogs. *ASCD Education Update*, 60(2). Retrieved from http://www.ascd.org/publications/newsletters/education-update/feb18/vol60/num02/Why-Schools-Are-Going-to-the-Dogs.aspx

U.S. Department of Justice, (2011). *Americans with Disabilities Act*. Retrieved from https://www.ada.gov/service_animals_2010.htm

EXTENSION ACTIVITIES

Discussion Questions

1. ADA states that allergies or a fear of dogs is not an acceptable reason for a service dog to not be allowed on premises. Could this be an example of discrimination? If a person has a real, intensive fear of dogs, could having an animal that they are deathly afraid of in the same room cause the individual to have a form of a "disability" in a sense? What about the child with severe allergies who begins to have labored breathing and contracts hives just from exposure to pet dander?
    a. Discuss how you would solve this problem if you were a school administrator.
    b. How will you ensure that you are not putting one person's needs over another's?
    c. Identify what laws you are abiding by or that are supporting your decisions.
2. How does a school district determine whether an animal is being used for service or support?
    a. Explain how you would determine this if you were the one making the decision.
3. Could a case be made for the use of either a support or service animal and the importance/need of their function? Explain you answer.

4. Research the use of therapy dogs by school staff. Do the benefits of having an animal present in schools outweigh the potential disadvantages? Explain your answer.

Write a Letter Assignment

Pick a side:

Write a letter from a parent's view to your child's school administrator outlining the reasons why your child should have a service animal with him or her throughout the school day.

Write a letter from a parent's view opposing having a service animal present in your child's classroom.

Discussion Paper

After reading this chapter, find a minimum of two additional articles that support this topic and write a double-spaced discussion paper following APA guidelines, including a bibliography page, to address the following:

- Before reading this chapter, my opinion on this issue was _____.

- In your own words, what is the issue at hand?

- Analyze what you see as the two sides of this issue.

- Identify a perceived misconception from either side. (When doing this, list the actual sentence(s) or portion of the sentence, citing the page number that you are making reference to, then write your response as to why you think it is a misconception. The key word is "perceived.")

- And finally, which side do you personally agree with more and why? (Refer to your personal experiences, here. If you have dealt with this issue in your personal life, work, teaching, etc., include that information in your answer.)

- Make sure to include in-text citations (when appropriate) from the supporting articles that you found.

Chapter 10

Assistive Technology
Is It Changing General Education?

Vaughn L. Bicehouse

PICTURE THIS: It's Friday evening and you are attending your child's home football game at the local high school stadium. You are seated in the family section, and beside your family is a young man in a high-powered wheelchair using a very expensive computer-based communication device. You overhear the mom telling the dad that this system should be updated so that their son can feel more included in the football game. Dad agrees and suggests that they contact the school to provide a newer version of the child's assistive technology. Your group begins a discussion on the issue—some people in support of it, some indifferent, and some totally against the expense of elaborate assistive equipment since the local taxpayers are footing the bill for this student.

What Is the Issue?

Assistive technologies—are they best used in special education classrooms or are they more appropriate in general education settings? Assistive technology has been an important part of many children with disabilities' daily routines. Special educators, paraprofessionals, and support staff have been on the frontlines of implementing assistive technology to help students with individualized education programs (IEPs) access the curriculum and provide specially designed instruction.

Years of using assistive technology by special education teachers and support staff have enabled students with disabilities to bypass their educational weaknesses and augment their individual strengths. Often assistive technology is implemented with universal design for learning (UDL) to present information in learning formats that accommodate individual needs of students. Assistive technology, when used properly, can be a beneficial tool to help students better understand the curriculum by providing tutorials, simulations, and problem-solving activities.

One of the conundrums of employing assistive technology is the fact that the teachers and students must have a solid background with assistive technology so students can flourish in their learning environments. This requires consistent training, monitoring, and direct instruction that has been a cornerstone of special education programming.

When the Individuals with Disabilities Education Act (IDEA) was reauthorized in 1997, it mandated that the possibility of assistive technology be considered for every child with an IEP. If the IEP team deemed it essential, students who had often been in less integrated special education classrooms would now need their assistive technology to follow them in general education classrooms and settings. To work, this means that general education teacher's attitudes, comfort level, training, and level of competence in the use of assistive technology could either make or mar the process of technological integration. This fact leaves many teachers asking what assistive technology is and how its use by students with disabilities will change the dynamics of the classroom.

Assistive technologies (AT) in their simplest form are equipment designed to help individuals function in their environment. Hersh and Johnson (2008) define assistive technologies as the equipment, devices, apparatus, services, systems, processes, and modifications made to the environment for use by people with disabilities. Winter & O'Raw (2010), define them as the equipment, tools and product systems used to empower interactions for people with disabilities. According to Lancioni, Sigafoos, O'Reilly, and Singh (2013), assistive technologies are various devices with the aim of helping persons with special educational/rehabilitation needs better function in daily life. Bouck (2017) states that assistive technologies give people with disabilities access to a whole new environment, so they can live life to the fullest and attain a higher quality of life.

Many children and adults use assistive technology for a range of health, education, employment, and participation outcomes. Both children and adults who use assistive technology must become competent in its use. This can be a challenge because of everchanging advances in the field of science and technology. New technology can be expensive and tricky to implement. Indeed, these two factors are constantly examined and debated when the issue of AT is addressed in school and society at large.

Assistive technology can be divided into two primary categories: low tech and high tech. Low technology is generally done without the purchase of expensive materials and does not require an intense level of training. Because of the simplicity of the materials, adjustments can be made easily when necessary. A few examples of low-tech equipment include the use of a pencil grip, finger grip ruler, large grid chart paper, and a corner rounding punch.

High-tech equipment is usually more expensive and must be purchased. Often training is needed for the student using it, as well as for the teachers, professionals, and support staff working with the child. However, with the increased use of technology in everyday life, these devices will often allow the user to easily blend in with everybody else. Some examples of high-tech devices include electronic tablets, augmentative communication devices, motorized wheelchairs, and smart boards. It should be noted that the choice between high-tech and low-tech options depends on the individual student and his or her need for specialized assistive technology.

What Does the Law Say?

The Technology-Related Assistance for Individuals Act of 1988 (P.L. 100–407) was the first federal effort to develop a "consumer-responsive" comprehensive program for the selection and delivery of assistive technology devices and services for individuals of all ages with disabilities (Committee on Education Labor, 2018). This act made available to states, through the Department of Education, federally backed grant monies to create formal systems to provide assistive technological services to people with disabilities at no cost to the families. States developed model delivery systems to promote awareness, training, and access to assistive technology.

Assistive technology devices and services were first circumscribed in federal law in the Individuals with Disabilities Education Act (IDEA) of 1990 (Public Law 101–476). The legal cornerstone for providing assistive technology devices and services is found in Section 300.105 in the Federal Register based on the most recent re-authorization of IDEA. IDEA Part B quantifies that individual education program (IEP) teams consider assistive technology for students with disabilities if it helps them access the curriculum.

On a case-by-case basis, the use of school-purchased assistive technology devices in a child's home or in other settings is required if the child's IEP team determines that the child needs access to those devices to receive a free and appropriate public education (FAPE).

These definitions remained unchanged until 2004 with the passage of the Individuals with Disabilities Education Improvement Act (Public Law 108–446) when an exemption to the definition of an assistive technology device was added to clarify a school system's responsibility to provide surgically implanted technology such as cochlear implants.

How Does This Affect Schools?

Since districts must consider whether a child with a disability needs assistive technology, school districts must be knowledgeable about the range of technologies to best support their students. In 1997, the widely accepted Chamber model asks that IEP teams consider the following questions for students who may need AT:

1. What do we want the students to do with the curriculum?
2. In which educational undertakings (reading, writing, listening, math, movement, sitting, seeing, self-care, transitioning, etc.) are the students unable to partake?

3. Will assistive technologies be able to support the achievement of these objectives?
4. What has been done to meet the needs for special education?
5. Do we as an IEP team have adequate knowledge about assistive technologies?
6. Under what conditions, environment(s), and for how long should the implementation be performed?
7. What has already taken place in the environment, technology, and process?

In 2012, Douglas, Wojcik and Thompson expanded the Chambers model to include the effective use of AT to support students' functional skills such as reading, communication, movement, and so on. In addition, they note that assistive technology is "not specific" to one foreseen group of disabilities or one foreseen skill. Being acutely aware of many of the concerns about assistive technologies, Douglas, Wojcik and Thompson (2012) also advocated using low-cost and user friendly low technologies first before considering high-cost technologies in educational settings. IEP teams with this in mind need to effectively collaborate with teachers, school personnel, assistive technology specialists, and other stakeholders to ensure learners are getting appropriate AT services.

What Is the Impact on Students Needing Special Education or 504 Plan Services?

Students with IEPs and 504 plan service agreements have the right to a public education that is both accessible and free from discrimination. Accommodations, aids, and services must be provided to students who have an IEP or 504 plan to provide them with equity and equal participation in academic and nonacademic activities. Many students with disabilities because of their developmental challenges need help to function to their maximum potential in public school settings. The use of assistive technology can be a useful tool in supporting these students.

If the IEP or 504 team agrees that assistive technologies are needed, they are provided by the child's home school district at no cost to the student's family. Moreover, if a student needs the AT to complete academic tasks at home or in the community the student has the right to take the assistive technology with him or her when he or she leaves school. Although the law requires districts to provide the assistive technology needed by students, there are issues that arise with the process.

With the proper training and support, students can use AT to be independent and navigate their school environment. A lack of support and training can lead to stressors for students and teachers alike. Why would schools not fully back the effective use of AT? There are several reasons this occurs: (a) There is a lack of comfort by administrators and teachers with technology, (b) the teachers and professional staff are not properly trained to help and support students who use AT, (c) assistive technology readiness assessments are not used to guide service planning for students, (d) AT is not adapted to a student's needs and context in varied settings throughout the school day, and (e) cost-driven concerns trump best practices. High-end technology can be very costly (i.e. power chairs and some augmentative communication devices). Because AT is as varied as the needs of the students who use it, it is critically important to have it implemented effectively to help students feel empowered and confident in their learning environment.

What Is the Impact on Students in General Education?

According to the National Education Association, the number of students receiving special education services has risen 30% since 2005. Seventy-five percent of these students spend all or part of their day in general education classrooms. The growing rates of students with IEP's in general education classrooms on a daily basis means that more students than ever before are now using assistive technology (Okolo & Diedrich, 2014). The prevalence rates, however, vary and often reflect specific disability groups. Accordingly, rates fluctuate by age and low and high incidence disabilities. Bouck (2016) estimates that less than 25% of students with low incidence disabilities use AT and less than 10% of students with high incidence disabilities use AT.

The use of AT in general education means that students with disabilities can participate in natural environments. Students using AT are full-fledged members of general education classes, and teachers must collaborate and provide support for the students placed in their care. The law mandates that students with disabilities are educated whenever possible with their typical peers. Assistive technology enables these students to access grade-level content that may not have been available to them in the past.

Inclusion of students using AT results in a better education for all students. All students get to see the benefits of assistive technology in the context of the least restrictive environment. In addition, students, teachers, and technology support staff become more involved in the process of bringing technology into the classroom, which bolsters independence and skill mastery with little to no assistance.

Conclusion

The appropriate use of assistive technology is important for children and adults alike. Environments that were once inaccessible to some individuals with disabilities are now unconfined and attainable due to assistive technology. Technology provides great potential for students with disabilities to communicate and become more efficient in the classroom.

Federal law ensures that students who need AT to be successful in the classroom have it provided for use in school, at home, and the community. Technology has a great impact on the lives of children with communication, physical disabilities, and functional limitations. No doubt technological advances will continue at a remarkable rate in the coming years, and the diversity, availability, and use of assistive devices will increase as well.

References

Bouck, E. C. (2016). A national snapshot of assistive technology for students with disabilities. *Journal of Special Education Technology*, 31(1), 4–13. doi:10.1177/0162643416633330

Bouck, E. C. (2017). *Assistive technology.* Thousand Oaks, CA: SAGE.

Committee on Education Labor (2018). Retrieved from https://www.congress.gov/committee/house-education-and-labor/hsed00?q=%7B%22committee-activity%22%3A%22hsed00Hearings+by%22%

Douglas, K., & Wojcik, B., & Thompson, J. (2012). Is there an app for that? *Journal of Special Education Technology*, 27(2), 59–70.

Hersh, M., & Johnson, M. (Eds.). (2008). *Assistive technology for visually impaired and blind people.* London, UK: Springer-Verlag.

Lancioni, G. E., Sigafoos, J., O'Reilly, M. F., & Singh. N. B. (2013). Defining assistive technology and the target populations. In J. L. Matson (Ed)., Assistive technology: Interventions for Individuals with Severe/Profound and Multiple Disabilities (pp. 1–7). New York, NY: Springer. Retrieved from http://link.springer.com/chapter/ 10.1007/978-1-4614-4229-5_1/fulltext.htm

Okolo, C. M. & Diedrich, J. (2014). Twenty-five years later: How is technology used in the education of students with disabilities? Results of a Statewide Study. *Journal of Special Education Technology*, 29(1), Retrieved from https://www.learntechlib.org/p/130509/

Winter, E., & O'Raw, P. (2010). *Literature review of the principles and practices relating to inclusive education for children with special educational needs.* Trim, Northern Ireland: National Council for Special Education.

EXTENSION ACTIVITIES

Discussion Questions

1. Technology is in a constant state of flux and growth. Most certainly students with communication and developmental disabilities benefit from these changes. As more and more assistive technology devices become part of these students' daily lives (often starting in preschool) parents, school administrators, and teachers must become sophisticated consumers and expert practitioners.

a. Discuss how you could help parents who may be looking for assistive technology for their son or daughter.

b. How would you as a school administrator balance the AT needs of each student with the fiscal constraints of the school budget?

c. As a teacher, who will you utilize to provide objective evaluations of new equipment? In addition, how will you receive the training you need to effectively support each student's specially designed AT instruction?

2. How have federal laws evolved regarding the topic of assistive technologies?

a. Explain why the numbers of students using AT are still quite low.

3. Why would some general education teachers be reluctant to have students who need assistive technology in their classroom? Explain your answer.

4. List some current technological advances that help students with disabilities. Explain your answer citing low-cost and high-cost assistive technology devices and apps.

Rubric Assignment

To graduate from sixth grade and move to junior high school, each student must present a culminating project about what they've learned from grades one through six.

You as the teacher must create a rubric to assess the students. The rubric must account for the students in your general education class who use assistive technology to communicate.

The rubric has the following areas for assessment: language/presentation, main ideas, visual aids, evidence of growth, and technology. Create at least three sub-categories for each area and a checklist with numeric values for each section.

Visual Display

The junior high school where you teach is holding an open house for parents, school board members, and community participants. You have been asked by your building principal (LEA) to work with your school's technology specialist and set-up a booth highlighting assistive technology that is used in your building. Consequently, your principal requests a visual display using Pinterest, Prezi, or a Vheme template of your choice to review before you set up your stand.

- Create the visual display that will be turned in to your LEA.

- Highlight low technology and high technology that is being used by students in your building.

- Showcase current apps that can benefit and support students whose disability adversely affects their educational performance in the general education classroom.

- Colorfully demonstrate that creativity and individualization are the keys to the successful use of assistive technology.

Assistive Technology K-W-L Form

After reading the chapter and independently researching and reading three to five current, peer-reviewed journal articles on assistive technology, create a K-W-L chart that demonstrates your understanding of AT. The first column details what you now *know* about assistive technology. The second column details what you *want* to know about assistive technology. The third column highlights current trends and issues that you have *learned* about assistive technology that can help you in the classroom.

Brainstorming Solutions

Create a web diagram that generates 10–15 potential solutions for a student who has issues with reading, talking, and connecting in a general education classroom. All the solutions need to include at least one example of a high technology or low technology that might address the child's deficit with reading, talking, or connecting. If possible, share your findings with another student in your class.

Discussion Paper

After reading this chapter, find a minimum of two additional articles that support this topic and write a double-spaced discussion paper following APA guidelines, including a bibliography page, to address the following:

- Before reading this chapter, my opinion on this issue was _____.

- In your own words, what is the issue at hand?

- Analyze what you see as the two sides of this issue.

- Identify a perceived misconception from either side. (When doing this, list the actual sentence(s) or portion of the sentence, citing the page number that you are making reference to, then write your response as to why you think it is a misconception. The key word is "perceived.")

- And finally, which side do you personally agree with more and why? (Refer to your personal experiences, here. If you have dealt with this issue in your personal life, work, teaching, etc., include that information in your answer.)

- Make sure to include in-text citations (when appropriate) from the supporting articles that you found.

Chapter 11

504 Service Agreement
Is This More Appropriate Than an IEP for a Student with a Disability?

Vaughn L. Bicehouse

PICTURE THIS: It's the third month of school and most of your second graders have gotten into the routine of a typical school day. For the most part they've gotten used to having you for their teacher and are now acquainted with the classroom norms, procedures, and routines. However, one child in particular is not catching on to routines like the others. Johnny is your challenging child. From the moment he enters the room he pokes students trying to hang up their coats and has trouble finding his cubby. Accordingly, he can't find the materials he needs in his desk and book bag, blurts out answers, has difficulty following directions, seldom completes homework, and at recess runs, pushes other children, argues, throws temper tantrums, and if not watched will climb up trees. To say the least you're exasperated and talked with both the guidance counselor and his parent. You're starting to think Johnny may need special adaptations and accommodations. Your conundrum is does he qualify for an IEP, a 504 service agreement, or is he just a very active child?

What Is the Issue?

504 service agreement. Individualized education program (IEP). What is the difference between the two and do students with disabilities qualify for both? There is a difference between the two documents because both came out of two different pieces of educational legislation. The Rehabilitation Act of 1973 (PL 93–112) predated the Individuals with Disabilities Education Act. Teachers, parents, school administrators and professionals who work with students in public schools need a keen understanding of both to help their students with disabilities be successful in achieving their potential in school.

The Rehabilitation Act of 1973, Section 504 states:

> No otherwise qualified individual with a disability in the United States ... shall, solely by reason of his or her disability, be excluded from the participation in, be denied the benefits of, or be subjected to discrimination under any program or activity receiving federal financial assistance.

Indeed, this was a civil rights law that protected the rights of a student with a disability in public school settings. The law provided for accommodations to minimize the impact of a child's disability. Section 504 defines disability in broad terms. Therefore, it allows students with disabilities to qualify for accommodations even if their academic performance is not "significantly delayed. Section 504 requires the general education system to support students who need adaptations and accommodations to benefit from their educational experience.

The Education for All Handicapped Children Act and its amendments are antidiscrimination laws that protect school-aged children so that they receive an appropriate education in public school. Now known as IDEA, the law requires special education services to be provided for students if their disability "adversely affects" their educational performance. The law has become increasingly detailed and prescriptive and since the Endrew decision (2017) requires school districts to provide students with disabilities the chance to make meaningful "appropriately ambitious" progress in school. A student with a disability may qualify for an IEP, a 504 agreement, or both.

What Does the Law Say?

The Rehabilitation Act, passed in 1973, prohibits discrimination against individuals with disabilities by entities that receive federal tax monies such as hospitals, universities and public schools. This law was enacted to guarantee equal opportunities for all students, with or without a disability. It champions the notion that a student with a disability be included in general education. School-aged children who qualify under Section 504 are guaranteed the right to a free and appropriate education. Indeed, they have the right to be included in both education and extracurricular activities (Davis, 2016).

For many years Section 504 was disregarded by most school personnel because they believed that all children who had a disability had their needs covered by IDEA. Section 504 defines disability in a broader way than IDEA. Now more than ever parents are looking to schools to provide 504 service agreements because IDEA does not cover students whose disability does not "significantly impact" their educational performance.

Section 504 service agreements give the students who are not covered under IDEA the accommodations and modifications they need in general education settings. The rationale for each accommodation and modification must be explicit and is spelled out in the 504 service agreement. If a student with a visual impairment needs preferential seating, then that is stated clearly in the plan. If these accommodations are not met, then the district is breaking the federal law and consequences will ultimately be determined. Many times, students start out with 504 service agreements and down the road their disability starts to affect their educational performance to a greater degree. At this point they are tested for special education services under IDEA. Undeniably the Rehabilitation Act and IDEA are similar because they protect students with disabilities in schools; however, IDEA affords much more support and specialized instruction.

Upon having reason to suspect that a child may be eligible under IDEA, a district must secure a parent's consent for testing and complete evaluation procedures in a reasonable period that is consistent with state timelines. This is true even if the child already had a 504 service agreement. If the multidisciplinary team (MDT) determines the child is exceptional and meets the qualifications for one of the 13 categories, then the IEP team will meet to plan services as mandated by IDEA. Special education services are provided without cost to the student and family with the least restrictive environment being the first option unless the severity of the disability prohibits that placement.

According to IDEA, special education is first and foremost individualized instruction. It is designed to address the unique needs of students with disabilities and help them achieve their maximum potential. The primary vehicle for designing each student's program is their individualized education plan (IEP). Children with IEPs also have the right to appropriate identification and educational services, necessary related services, least restrictive environment, and notification and procedural rights to parents on behalf of their children.

How Does This Affect Schools?

Now that the educational theory of inclusion is prevalent in today's public schools, it is critical for districts to know the major legal and policy foundations for inclusive practices. Schools must account for potential ways to deliver appropriate public education in the least restrictive environment for students with disabilities. The law is clear that these students need their differing abilities addressed in curriculum, instruction, assessment, and transitional skills. Consequently, the general education classroom must be looked at as the first placement option and the least restrictive environment for students with disabilities. Both Section 504 of the Rehabilitation Act and IDEA have stringent federal and state guidelines that must be followed by school districts.

Section 504 requires that an official notice and consent for a 504 evaluation be sent to parents with an informational packet informing them of their rights. Once the parents grant consent, the 504 team must find evidence of the student's disability and determine if the disability is keeping the student from performing to his or her potential. The 504 team is usually made up of a Local Education Agency (LEA) representative, a general education teacher, a case administrator, a school psychologist, a nurse, and any other individual with expertise regarding the student and his or her disability (Black & Koziol, 2012). The feedback from the parents and health professionals is also important for a plan to be written and implemented. IDEA also mandates strong parent involvement.

IDEA requires school districts to collaborate with parents as equal partners in the design and implementation of educational programs, services, and supports for students with disabilities. IDEA focuses on child find, eligibility, and FAPE when establishing whether a child "thought to be exceptional" qualifies for services. Like 504 teams, the multidisciplinary team must get a parent's consent to complete an evaluation for IEP services.

For eligibility the requisite team must determine, based on a variety of sources in the evaluation, whether the student meets the conditions for one or more of IDEA's specified classifications, and if so whether the child has a resulting need for special education. If the child qualifies for special education, by law, the IEP team must develop an IEP that is appropriate for the specific needs of the child. Indeed, it must be appropriate for the individual student in accordance with prescribed procedures and, at last, is reasonably designed to provide a meaningful benefit to the child.

What Is the Impact on Students Needing Special Education or 504 Plan Services?

Both 504 service agreement plans and IEPs serve students with disabilities. Sometimes the areas they cover overlap, but a primary difference is that Section 504 states that districts must make "reasonable accommodations for students" and IEPs (since the *Endrew* decision) must make "meaningful progress" for each child with an IEP.

Section 504 protections are broad and cover a lot of school-aged children. This allows for children whose disability impacts one or more major life activities to qualify for accommodations, even if their academic performance is not delayed to the point that they need special education. Most frequently, students with ADHD and chronic conditions such as HIV/AIDS, hepatitis, tuberculosis, Acute Flaccid Myelitis (AFM) virus, and other medical conditions (e.g., diabetes, epilepsy, cancer, allergies, and asthma) are eligible under Section 504.

Although Section 504 enables many students with disabilities the option of a 504 service agreement plan, it does not compel schools to provide significant or expensive services. The 504 service agreements are to provide "reasonable modifications and accommodations" in general education settings. This may include special assistance with a service animal or help from a paraprofessional, a behavior management plan, medication monitoring, or the provision of special study or quiet areas or assistive technology devices.

504 service agreement plans may also qualify a student, especially a student with serious health issues, shortened school days, online education, rest periods throughout the school day, and/or modified physical education curriculum or activities. In addition, some students

may also receive related services such as speech/language pathology, occupational or physical therapy or counseling, or even drug and alcohol counseling. Funding for students with 504 service agreements typically comes from the school's general education fund, not special education funding.

Students who qualify for IEPs receive an entire network of services to meet their individual needs. Unlike Section 504, IDEA provides federal financial assistance to state and local education agencies to guarantee special education and related services to eligible children with disabilities. IEPs are required to contain the following six items for every child.

1. A statement of the student's present level of functioning. This statement should be a description of what the student can do; what skills the student has in academic, social, behavioral, and communication skills; and the curriculum areas that the student needs to continue to show progress and growth.

2. A list of the annual goals, including benchmarks or short-term objectives, that address the student's needs in general education settings and curriculum.

3. A specific list of the supplementary aids and services that are needed by the student to achieve his or her goals, benchmarks, and short-term objectives.

4. An explanation of the extent, if any, to which the student will not participate in the general education classroom and in other activities with students without disabilities.

5. A description of any testing accommodations that the student needs to participate in state- or district-wide assessments.

6. A description of the student's progress to be sent home regularly to the student's parents or guardians.

Revisions to IDEA, coupled with recent U.S. Supreme Court decisions, have changed how IEPs are designed for students in three critical ways. First, IEP teams must address specifically how a student's disability affects his or her involvement and advancement in the general education curriculum. Quantifiable goals and objectives must be written, even when students are being measured with alternate achievement standards. Additionally, specific modifications, accommodations, and supports are to be noted, which demonstrates that to the "maximum extent" students are exposed to and working toward mastery of general education goals and standards. No longer is it acceptable for students to make adequate progress now that their IEPs should give the student the opportunity to "meet challenging objectives" (Davis, 2016). To ensure that this is occurring, students with IEPs are included alongside their peers without disabilities in formal and informal assessment procedures.

Second, IDEA mandates that all students, even students with severe disabilities, be included in state and district assessments to gage how well they are performing with and to what extent they are learning based on the instruction that is being given to them. Assessment results need to be connected to instruction and clearly delineated and explained to parents or guardians at an IEP meeting.

Third, when alternate assessments are used (as indicated in a student's IEP) the assessments must to the greatest extent possible align with grade-level content standards and assessments. Students with IEPs have an absolute right to a free and appropriate education in the least restrictive environment. This does not mean that the LRE for every child is the general education classroom. Whereas access to the general education curriculum may be easier to achieve in a general education classroom, this is not a prerequisite to general curriculum access. Additionally, students with IEPs have transition goals and real-life authentic instructional opportunities and methods for helping teach them academic, social, and behavioral content.

As more students are being identified as needing special services, 504 service agreements and IEPs have taken on greater significance. The momentum toward full inclusion is a balancing act as public schools embrace a diverse population of students. As student profiles continue to change and evolve, effective practitioners' collective expertise must be utilized and shared to provide successful inclusive schooling. Such student diversity requires teachers who have the needed skills to meet the unique needs and challenges of their students with disabilities as well as their students who do not.

What Is the Impact on Students in General Education?

Not so long ago students with disabilities were educated in separate schools, separate classrooms, using specialized materials, and trained by special education teachers. Today 57% of students with disabilities spend more than 80% of their day in general education classrooms, although general education teachers report that that they lack the knowledge, skills, and expertise to effectively instruct diverse learners (Blanton, Pugach, & Florian, 2011). Moreover, many of the teachers felt that providing the supports and accommodations to their students with disabilities "took them away" from time they could have spent working on foundational skills with students without disabilities. Nevertheless, students without disabilities do not have special rights in general education.

Highly trained teachers are needed to ensure the success of all students assigned to their care. Indeed, the diversity of today's students poses a plethora of opportunities for teachers to facilitate positive peer interactions and relationships. Providing a rich and appropriate education helps all students acquire academic skills and understand intricate stimuli. General education teachers can foster a caring community within their classroom that promotes a sense of belonging—where all students are valued regardless of abilities and needs and are able to participate and contribute.

Some schools are starting to incorporate more cooperative learning and peer support groups. This would affect all students within this setting, not just those with IEPs or 504 service agreements.

As peers are increasingly involved in providing support strategies, they are learning important lessons about advocacy. Consequently, it is not uncommon to have peers without disabilities attend 504, IEP, individualized transition planning (ITP), and other planning meetings to advocate for their friends with disabilities. Progressive schools and classrooms can institute educational service delivery models that reflect the worldview that all children belong and diversity is to be celebrated, fostered, and encouraged.

Conclusion

In summary, there are two types of plans that service students with disabilities in public schools. These are 504 service agreements and individualized education programs (IEPs). Both documents guarantee that children receive the educational and related services they need to be successful. Each of these management tools guides the educational system as it plans for and delivers an appropriate education to students who are protected by antidiscrimination laws.

References

Black, K., & Koziol, K. (PowerPoint presenters). (2012, October 23). Section 504 keys to implementation in Prince Williams County Public Schools. Manassas, VA.

Blanton, L. P., Pugach, M. C., & Florian, L. (2011). *Preparing general education teachers to improve outcomes for students with disabilities*. Washington, DC: American Association of Colleges for Teacher Education & National Center for Learning and Disabilities.

Davis, L. J. (2016). Introduction: Disability, normality, and power. In L. J. Davis (Ed.), The disability studies reader (5th ed.) (pp. 2–4). London, UK: Taylor and Francis.

McKibben, S. (2018). Why schools are going to the dogs. *ASCD Education Update, 60*(2). Retrieved from http://www.ascd.org/publications/newsletters/education-update/feb18/vol60/num02/Why-Schools-Are-Going-to-the-Dogs.aspx

EXTENSION ACTIVITIES

Discussion Questions

1. Richard transferred schools before the start of the new school year. He is a student who is profoundly deaf and uses a sign language interpreter, FM system, and preferential seating at his last school. His

grades were sent to his new school but no 504 agreement or IEP were received. His parents want him placed in the fifth grade general education classroom and expect his new school to have everything in place in less than 2 weeks before the new school year begins. What should be done (if anything) to provide Richard with an appropriate education and smooth transition to his new school?

    a. Discuss how you would solve this problem if you were a school administrator or teacher leader.

    b. How will you ensure you are not putting one student's needs over another's when working with Richard in the classroom setting?

    c. Identify what laws you are abiding by or that are supporting your decisions.

2. How does the district determine if Richard qualifies for a 504 service agreement or an IEP?

    a. Explain how you would determine this if you were the one making the decision.

3. As his general education teacher, what do you think would be most appropriate for Richard, a 504 service agreement or an IEP? Explain you answer.

Write a Letter Assignment

Pick a side:

> Write a letter from a parent's view to your child's school administrator outlining the reasons why your child should have a 504 service agreement.

> Write a letter from a parent's view to your child's school administrator outlining the reasons why your child should have an IEP.

Discussion Paper

After reading this chapter, find a minimum of two additional articles that support this topic and write a double-spaced discussion paper following APA guidelines, including a bibliography page, to address the following:

- Before reading this chapter, my opinion on this issue was _____.

- In your own words, what is the issue at hand?

- Analyze what you see as the two sides of this issue.

- Identify a perceived misconception from either side. (When doing this, list the actual sentence(s) or portion of the sentence, citing the page number that you are making reference to, then write your response as to why you think it is a misconception. The key word is "perceived.")

- And finally, which side do you personally agree with more and why? (Refer to your personal experiences, here. If you have dealt with this issue in your personal life, work, teaching, etc., include that information in your answer.)

- Make sure to include in-text citations (when appropriate) from the supporting articles that you found.

Conceptual Organization Assignment

Concept maps can outline and connect facts, giving the learner the chance to view and study information at a quick glance. Create a concept map for a 504 service agreement plan and an IEP.

Self-assessment form:

Design your own self-assessment form that answers the following two questions regarding a 504 service agreement plan versus an IEP.

1. Before I learned about_____, I thought_____.
2. Now, I know_____.

Brain-based learning assignment:

Authentic instruction takes place when the brain connects new knowledge to old. Students associate what they are learning—new knowledge—to what they already comprehend—prior knowledge. Because the brain is constantly making sense of new patterns of learning it is critical for teachers and students alike to collaborate and discuss out loud what is being taught. For this assignment you're to work with two or three classmates (if applicable, if not, do this independently) and comprise a list of reasonable accommodations and modifications for the new student you will be sharing in your general education classrooms.

Things to consider regarding the student: what grade level is he or she; his or her disability; if he or she has a 504 service agreement plan or an IEP; what instructional prompts would best serve the student with acquisition, fluency, application, and generalization; and what supplementary aids and services might be needed in your general education setting.

Section VI

Transition Services

Chapter 12

Transition
Wouldn't All Students Benefit from a Transition Plan?

Jessica A. Hall-Wirth

PICTURE THIS: It's 8:30 on a Monday morning in October. You are a 12th-grader sitting in homeroom. Over the PA system, the secretary comes on and rattles off 15 public and private universities and colleges that will be visiting next Friday and how to sign up to meet with them. Immediately, your stomach starts to churn and panic begins to set in. You begin to think, "Should I have already committed to a college?" "What if college isn't the path I want to take?" "What are my options?" Students are faced with many decisions upon completion of high school. Should they have to do this alone?

What Is the Issue?

Transitions represent a major shift in the daily context for adolescents to interact and transitions are often times underestimated. For some students, transitions are smooth and peaceful, while for others it can be daunting and stressful. School transitions are related to a variety of behavioral and psychological changes. For many students, the transition from high school into college can be more stressful than the transition to kindergarten or to high school. Some students attend 2-year community colleges, whereas others attend 4-year colleges or universities. Some may bypass college altogether and go directly into their chosen career, while others may attend a vocational or training program. The transition into college, a training facility, or the workplace for many students represents the first time they simultaneously live away from home. If going directly to college, many students do not adapt well to college life and experience academic difficulties during their first year of school, which can eventually lead to dropping out (Tinto, 2006).

Transitions can be a difficult time in any child or adolescent's life. Making these types of decisions is not easy for anyone, but why are adolescents often times making these emotional decisions alone? Researchers have found that adults can use rational processes when facing emotional decisions, but teenager's brains are simply not yet equipped to think through things the same way (Talukder, 2013). The fact that the decision-making centers of the brain continue to develop well into the early 20s could offer educators insight on how to support students during this transitional phase. Currently, school districts are allocating resources toward counseling programs that help support students and families regarding issues such as conducting the college search, testing, application procedures, and so on. Researchers have suggested that the most well-adjusted students are the ones who demonstrate a sense of being part of the school community. Although there are a percentage of students who are able (with support) to make rational decisions and take the next steps toward transition, there is a large majority who struggle. Consequently, the question arises, "Wouldn't a transition plan benefit all students?"

What Does the Law Say?

The Individuals with Disabilities Education Act of 2004, also known as IDEA, has specific guidelines that ensure all children (ages 3 to 21) with disabilities receive a free appropriate public education (FAPE). This specifically emphasizes that special education programming and related services must be appropriately designed to meet the unique needs for individuals with special needs and prepare them for future education, employment, and independent living. IDEA was originally mandated in 1975. When IDEA was reinstated in 2004, there were major changes made to the legal definition of "transition services." This new definition stated that the term "transition services" refers to a coordinated set of activities for a child with a disability that fulfill three requirements: (a) designed to be a results-oriented process, focused on improving not only academic achievement and functional achievement of the child with a disability to facilitate the child's movement from school to post-school activities; (b) based on the child's needs; and (c) includes instruction, related services, community experiences, the development of employment and other post-school adult living objectives, and when appropriate, acquisition of daily living skills and functional vocational evaluation (Wright & Wright, 2007). This new shift requires that transition services are based on the student's strengths, as well as their preferences and interests. This process ensures that the activities are designed to generate success for individuals. IDEA protects individuals with disabilities until they exit the high school setting. Upon graduation, the Rehabilitation Act of 1973 and the Americans with Disabilities Act (ADA) take over and protect individuals with special needs in the areas of employment, transportation, and public accommodations.

The Rehabilitation Act of 1973 requires individuals with disabilities the right to work in programming established by or receiving federal funding. Similarly, the Americans with Disabilities Act speaks directly within Title I, Title II, and Title III that no discrimination of any kind toward individuals with disabilities will be acceptable in employment, state, and local government, transportation services, or public accommodations. Therefore, individuals with disabilities must be treated fairly and equally in public spaces and employment.

How Does This Affect Schools?

With the establishment of IDEA, schools are required to follow a set of guidelines to ensure that all students with disabilities are provided with the appropriate education. IDEA requires public schools to provide a free and appropriate education in the least restrictive environment for individuals who are eligible for special education services. This, in turn, allows for students to be taught and have the ability to learn in a way that meets their individual needs. To ensure that these standards are being met, IDEA requires schools to develop an individualized education plan (IEP) for each child that specifies the special education criteria and related services that reflect the child's individualized needs.

The IEP cannot be developed by just anyone in the school. IDEA states that the IEP must be developed by a team of knowledgeable persons that are engaged with the child's education. This document must be reviewed annually by the team to adjust any goals, placement, or related services as the team sees fit. This team is made up of the child's special education teacher, general education teacher, parent(s), the child, if determined appropriate, an agency representative who is qualified to provide or supervise the provision of special education, and any other individuals at the parent's or agency's discretion.

Once the student turns 14 years of age in the state of Pennsylvania, the school district then becomes responsible for setting and aligning goals that fulfill the requirements of the transition plan. The transition plan is the heart of the transition process. The IEP team is required to develop goals that align with the student's future plans. To align these goals to the student's strengths and passions, the student will complete an interest inventory. These postsecondary goals are written by the IEP team and can be in one of four areas: (a) vocational training, (b) postsecondary education, (c) jobs and employment, and (d) independent living. Once the goals are set, it is the IEP team's job to decide what services the child will need to successfully meet his or her goals in the allotted time frame. Similar to the original IEP process, the transition services must be reviewed annually and updated to support the child's growth and success. If the school district does not follow through with the transition services listed in the IEP, then they are out of compliance.

What Is the Impact on Students Needing Special Education or 504 Plan Services?

Transition services have a great impact on students who receive special education. At the age of 14, when transition planning begins, the school district has the responsibility of not only helping to plan the child's future, but also implementing services to help the student reach those goals. Transition sets the stage for the rest of the individual's life. After high school, the protections and guarantees under IDEA no longer support or protect an individual. The laws govern that employers have to provide access to jobs and facilities, but there is limited individualized support.

During this transition period, there is a shift in the type of goals for which the student is striving. Students are now honing in on skills needed to complete their future job or to live independently. For example, if a student cannot independently tie his or her shoes, this may be a skill that will be worked on. School districts have been developing settings that allow for the students to generalize their skills in a "real" setting. School districts have been receiving grant funding that allow them to develop an apartment and/or coffee shop in their school. This provides the students with an opportunity to learn their skills needed and practice in a real-life setting. From here, students can transfer their skills to community-based programs. All of this is mandated to be executed for students receiving special education services.

If the school district does not provide these services for their special education students, it would be much more difficult for the student to live independently or even hold a job. For example, my brother has multiple disabilities and during high school he attended vocational training where he learned a series of job training skills that would allow him to apply to many different employers in our area. On a daily and consistent basis, he was held to high expectations regarding behavior, dress code, social skills, and work ethic. This allowed him to have constant support for 3 years leading up to graduation. With his transition plan, he then was provided the accommodations that he needed to be successful in the work place. Upon graduation, he had developed the skills that he needed to work independently. Without this transition plan, his skills would have been underdeveloped and he would not have found his purpose. School districts have a responsibility to prepare students for the next transition in their lives.

What Is the Impact on Students in General Education?

Currently, students in general education receive support from a school counselor or teacher in regard to how to apply for college, look for colleges, and what testing is needed. School counselors or teachers often times help general education students by providing resources and setting up colleges to come to campus to visit. But what about the students who don't know if college is for them or don't know their next steps? The 2017 unemployment rate for students who did not go to college after high school was 16.8% and, between 2016 and 2017, 530,000 young people dropped out of high school (Bureau of Labor Statistics, 2018). How should we, as educators, support these students to help them reach graduation and find a job?

The research is clear that transition plans have positively affected special education students. What if school districts developed a transition plan for all students? At this time the special education teacher, IEP team, and/or transition coordinator are the ones who are overseeing the transition plans and services. This would create overwhelming change in school districts in terms of workloads and staffing. General education teachers would then be responsible for helping general education students plan their future and align goals to help them achieve these goals.

Currently, the transition plans include postsecondary, vocational training, jobs, and employment and independent living goals. General education students may not need this level of support; it could be modified as per student need. With time, training, and a structured procedure, general education teachers could manipulate the current special education transition plan and make it fit for general education students. This would allow students to take control of their future and begin setting goals that would allow them to go in their new direction confidently. This extra step could help student retention and dropout rates and alleviate the emotional stress that comes with planning for the next phase of their lives.

Conclusion

In summary, the transitional period from high school to college or the work place can be a stressful time for students. Adolescents' brains have not yet fully developed in terms of their decision-making skills. Transition plans, a requirement by IDEA, allow students with disabilities to have support with developing and reaching goals connected to their future plans. These include independent living skills, jobs and employment, vocational training, and post-secondary education. The ADA and the Rehabilitation Act of 1973 support employment and public accommodations and services after high school. Transition plans are the first and final step for planning a student with special needs' future. There are many pros that allow students support and accommodations to reach their goals. Although this is always a work in progress, great strides are being made to help support students with disabilities after high school. The purpose of an IEP and transition plans are to support students and promote independence. As educators our goal is to provide the support and education necessary for all students to be able to be productive members of society once they've graduated.

References

Bureau of Labor Statistics (2018, April 26). *College enrollment and work activity of recent high school and college graduate summary*. Retrieved from https://www.bls.gov/news.release/hsgec.nr0.htm

Talukder, G. (2013). *Decision-making is still a work in progress for teenagers*. Retrieved from https://brainconnection.brainhq.com/2013/03/20/decision-making-is-still-a-work-in-progress-for-teenagers/

Tinto, V. (2006). Research and practice of student retention: What next? *Journal of College Student Retention, Research, Theory, and Practice*, 8(1), 1–19.

U.S. Department of Justice. (2009). A guide to disability rights law. Retrieved from https://www.ada.gov/cguide.htm#anchor64984

Wright, P.W. & Wright, P.D. (2007). Wrightslaw: Special Education Law, 2nd Edition Hartfield, VA:Harbor House Law Press, Inc.

EXTENSION ACTIVITIES

Discussion Questions

1. Think back to when you were 16 and making decisions regarding postsecondary education. Do you think you had the tools necessary to make a well-rounded decision regarding your transition to college or the work place?
   a. If so, what supports were in place at your high school to help you make this decision?
   b. If not, what resources did you utilize and adapt to help guide you to the decision that you made?

2. Do you feel that the generally accepted transition plan for students in special education would translate directly for a student who is not receiving special education services?
   a. If so, defend your reasoning.
   b. If not, what changes would you make to better serve the transition planning for a student not receiving special education services?

3. In a school district where funding may not be available to employ a transition coordinator, how would you as an administrator offer transition services to all students, whether general or special education students?

Transition Goal/Plan Activity

Think back to when you were 15 years old. What supports, resources, classes, and so on would have been beneficial to help you get to where you are today in terms of your career? Go to the pattan.net website and search "school-age special education forms." Look at a sample IEP (specifically the transition portion). Write up a transition plan for yourself, including goals, reso
urces, classes, support staff, and so on based on what is outlined on the IEP format.

Discussion Paper

After reading this chapter, find a minimum of two additional articles that support this topic and write a double-spaced discussion paper following APA guidelines, including a bibliography page, to address the following:

- Before reading this chapter, my opinion on this issue was _____.

- In your own words, what is the issue at hand?

- Analyze what you see as the two sides of this issue.

- Identify a perceived misconception from either side. (When doing this, list the actual sentence(s) or portion of the sentence, citing the page number that you are making reference to, then write your response as to why you think it is a misconception. The key word is "perceived.")

- And finally, which side do you personally agree with more and why: (Refer to your personal experiences, here. If you have dealt with this issue in your personal life, work, teaching, etc., include that information in your answer.)

- Make sure to include in-text citations (when appropriate) from the supporting articles that you found.

Section VII

Medical Needs

Chapter 13

Behavior Issues in Schools
Are Medications the Answer?

Eric J. Bieniek

PICTURE THIS: You are a teacher in an approved private school designed specifically for students with significant developmental and neurological diagnoses. A new student arrives to your life skills classroom. This is a student with significant social and pragmatic communication impairments. Consequently, this student has also developed a repertoire of problem behaviors that are described as significant and pervasive (verbal and physical aggression resulting in staff or student injury, property destruction, and elopement). Given the global needs of this student, he also sees a psychiatrist outside of the school setting and takes psychotropic medications at various times over the school day. Most recently, you have received a note from his mother and his new prescription bottle. She indicates that she would like this used in addition to his regular medications and that this is a sedative-type medication (Valium) to be utilized as needed (PRN) to address acute, significant behavioral episodes.

What Is the Issue?

There are a range of questions to consider so that the student's best interest remains a priority while still meeting the legal and ethical mandates that schools must follow regarding medication in the school setting. First, where are medications stored? Can a teacher keep medicines in the classroom? How safe is this option when we consider other students, professional staff, and even substitutes all coming and going throughout the average school day? Does the school need to designate a secured area for medicines? If you feel that these medicines should be stored securely, where exactly is that? This may include the nurse's, principal's or even a guidance counselor's office, but the question could then be one of access in an emergency or when a student is away from the building (field trips, recess).

Once we make sure items are safe, we now need to look at a plan for administering medications. The description of this situation is a volatile one when this student is upset. So, how do you give these medicines to the student? More specifically, who has the authority in a school setting such as this to approve using these medicines? The school in this scenario is an alternative education setting that has a range of professionals supporting students like this. This includes traditional school staff such as administrators, teachers, para-professionals, counselors, and school nurses. However, due to the therapeutic nature of the program, there is also a range of specialized services such as behavior specialists, a visiting psychiatrist, as well as speech, physical and occupational therapists. So, with all these skilled professionals, who makes the decision to provide the medications? Should it include only medical staff? Behavior specialists and counselors? Or is this a whole team consensus?

Another area to consider is when medicines are delivered, meaning what types of situations necessitate the provision of medication. Surely a classroom team would not provide medicines for every behavioral episode, but essentially, what types of episodes count? In this instance, a school team needs to develop a protocol that is consistent and in line with the overall goals of the student's behavioral support planning. A plan like this should include what types of behavior would constitute a safety issue significant enough to require medical intervention. This plan also should outline where medication administration is supported in an existing school or student specific crisis plan. In addition, the plan should also authorize the use of medicine in the actual and acute behavioral crisis. The school team also needs to decide how much and how often medicines can be offered. Is a decision like this more medically or educationally based? If medication is provided, what protocols or precautions need to be considered after administration, and what student behaviors need to be present for them to return to class? Should the student be sent home? Should he or she be sent to the hospital? What if the student or family does not agree with the school's decision to go home or to the hospital? Finally, what is the plan for the school, student, and family if providing medicine does not work effectively and a student continues to be agitated or the safety of those in the setting is still in question?

A school team also needs to have a plan for contacting the student's family and sharing information on incidents requiring medical intervention and tracking information (data) relevant to the school setting. This once again creates a need for effective protocols and assignment of responsibilities in the school setting. This includes assigning persons to make sure behavioral events requiring medicines are handled consistently and ensuring data are collected and disseminated effectively to families and medical providers in a manner that meets the needs of all parties. There also needs to be an ongoing mechanism to share information back and forth between the family, doctors, and school to share changes in dosages and side effects and ensure prescriptions are filled, available, and are providing the desired effects in a safe manner.

What Does the Law Say?

In a document titled "Guidelines for Pennsylvania Schools for the Administration of Medications and Emergency Care," developed by the Pennsylvania Department of Health and published in 2010, an explanation of state-level mandates and recommended practices is available regarding this very topic.

To summarize: "Guidelines for Pennsylvania Schools for the Administration of Medications and Emergency Care" are issued pursuant to 22 Pa. Code §12.41 (a), which requires school entities (defined as local public education providers, for example public schools, charter schools, cyber-charter schools, area vocational-technical schools, or intermediate units) to prepare written plans for the implementation of a comprehensive and integrated K–12 program of student services based on the needs of its students. The plan must include policies and procedures for emergency care and administration of medication and treatment, under the Controlled Substance, Drug, Device and Cosmetic Act (35 P.S. §§ 780–101–780–144) and guidelines issued by the Department of Health. The purpose of the guidelines is to help Pennsylvania schools ensure the safe and proper administration of medications to students (Pennsylvania Department of Health, 2010). This is a comprehensive guide to assisting access to medical supports and ensuring that all interventions falling within this area are carried in accordance to federal precedents such as the Rehabilitation Act of 1973 and IDEA, as well as state-level actions such as the Pharmacy Act, Medical Practice Act, Professional Nursing Law and Practical Nursing law. Throughout these laws, a focus is clearly placed on striking a balance between effective medical supports and ensuring an equal access to a fair and appropriate public education (FAPE). To achieve a balance between these equally significant variables a focus is provided on empowering school nurses to practice "prudently with the parameters of his or her nursing act," first (Pennsylvania Department of Health, 2010). However, when considering the situation at hand there is also a specific directive to nurses to "not engage in areas of highly specialized practice without adequate knowledge of the skills in the practice areas involved" (Pennsylvania Department of Health, 2010). This creates dissonance regarding roles and expertise in an approved private school setting where the students attending the school require a much wider range of "expertise" to support them effectively through the school day.

Obstacles highlighted in the school settings can include unlicensed school staff engaging in healthcare practices, occurrence of medication errors, misdiagnosis of acute or chronic conditions, heightened parent attention, securing controlled substances to avoid theft, and ongoing documentation omissions or inaccuracies. To address these barriers the Pennsylvania Department of Health recommends developing or realigning caseloads to meet the skill sets of professionals and hiring supplemental, licensed support staff. They also recommend collaborating with families to attempt to limit medication administration to at-home versus school and maintaining a pool of licensed substitute medical professionals to provide coverage during absences.

How Does This Affect Schools?

The potential for use of medication in schools is more prevalent than ever before, given a continued expectation for supported inclusion in today's public schools. As districts are scrambling to support the whole student, administrators and teachers are voicing genuine concerns around balancing mental health and character education along with rigorous academic and career preparation expectations. To efficiently support a student having mental health or behavioral concerns, the majority of clinical psychologists will tell you that a combination of effective one-to-one or group therapy and psychotropic medication is the best course to support students demonstrating problem behavior in the clinically significant range (Cardoso & Xavier, 2015). This dichotomy is one that requires comprehensive oversight and attention on the part of the professionals in the school setting. Who then is ultimately accountable to provide this care? Given the idiosyncratic nature of students who possess a mental health diagnosis and may demonstrate challenging behavior, the professional's responsible can vary from student to student and school to school. Professionals currently taking this responsibility on are already serving other, more traditional roles. Nonetheless, homeroom teachers, special-education teachers, school nurses, guidance counselors, IEP case managers, and even the school psychologist may be required to assume oversight of these services. Despite the variety of potential candidates, the most critical variable is that the student and his or her family trust this person and will be willing to collaborate efficiently as the team works through developing, executing, and then following an effective plan of care for the student. As we describe in the next section, while the obligations of those overseeing support of these students can be very individual, the process for assessment, intervention, and monitoring student progress follows a more systematic path, accomplished through individual education plans (IEPs) and Section 504 service agreements.

What Is the Impact on Students Needing Special Education or 504 Plan Services?

Public school educators most frequently utilize Section 504 service agreements and IEPs as a means to establish and monitor all forms of individualized supports for students. Supporting access to medical supports, such as medication, psychotropic or otherwise, would fall into this category as well.

In most public school settings, medication management and its oversight would fall to the medical experts in a school program, namely school nurses. It is then necessary to include nurses in the planning and monitoring processes in a meaningful way. In the scenario presented earlier, it may be the decision of the school nurse that delivering PRN medication for challenging behaviors is going beyond the normal expectations of an educational program. While a nurse's opinion is important in this process, the ultimate decision to support this type of intervention lies in the policy and procedure of the larger school district, which is often regulated by a board of school directors. This is unique and can be troublesome at times as you are essentially attempting to monitor a medically focused intervention in a system that is fundamentally focused on academics and career preparation.

So where is the middle ground? IEP and 504 plans can supply the means to define and support the provision of medical interventions, but it is especially important to understand that all educational systems will most certainly have variations in how they interpret and apply these plans. This may seem contrary to the original intentions of these federally mandated supports, but a range of variables, including student demographics, district resources, vision statements, legal precedents, and the availability (or lack thereof) to therapeutic services can all affect the final outcome of these plans and the interventions that accompany them. At the minimum, safety must be established for all parties. Optimally, IEP and 504 teams should also be collaborating with families and health care providers to monitor medication use and its results. To make this a reality, nurses (or other identified professionals) need to be actively communicating and sharing data with all team members to monitor medication use and effects. It is recommended that this be carried in a manner similar to the procedures for progress monitoring adopted for academic goals.

The impacts of medical supports in nontraditional settings like alternative education, partial hospitalization, or residential or in-patient school learning programs are different when compared to typical public education programs. This is due to the nature of the students supported in these programs. Access to a free and appropriate public education (FAPE) is a fundamental right for all students, even those having mental health concerns or challenging behaviors. Students having more severe or what is referred to as "clinically significant" diagnoses will often attend school in programs that are primarily therapeutic, while still providing quality educational opportunities. The support structures of nontraditional educational programs can vary greatly, from residential programing, in- or out-patient hospitalization, cyber-based programming, and full-time placement in an alternative school program.

Within the range of therapeutic interventions available to learners, professionals are still required to adhere to educational mandates described earlier, namely the IEP process and Section 504 supports. In an alternative education or partial mental health model, the opportunity for more traditional medical staffing (nursing and psychiatry) serves as a benefit in the scenario presented at the start of the chapter. Programs that are dually focused on delivering therapeutic and academic services require a more diverse range of support professionals to address the holistic needs of its learners. Having access to psychiatric nurses, psychologists, psychiatrists, licensed social workers and licensed counselors alleviates the need for oversight by one primary person—the school nurse—as we have referenced earlier in public education settings. This advantage is one that comes with consequences as well. Student's attending specialized educational programs are typically coming into school with pre-existing mental health and medical diagnoses, substance abuse, histories of abuse and/or trauma. Essentially, the resources available in these settings are most often necessary to support the presenting needs of these learners. Given the dynamic and multidisciplinary nature of these programs, the potential for effective collaboration and communication abounds but can also be confounded. Medication management and oversight is included as part of students' therapeutic treatment primarily but can also be accommodated and monitored procedurally through the students' IEPs.

IEPs for students having challenging behaviors, and attending alternative schools will additionally include explanations about ongoing treatment plans, the range of other therapies in use, family counseling, and community integration. It is through the elements contained in these holistic IEPs that an educational team can develop clear and objective criteria for use of medication. This includes protocols for when a medication is warranted, who makes those decisions, procedures to follow after medicines are used, and any other essential procedures to ensure dignity and safety. When plans like these are needed, having access to a multidisciplinary approach facilitates better comprehensive care where therapists can report changes in treatments, doctors can elicit feedback before and after dosage adjustments, and so on. Thus, in alternative and therapeutic programs, it appears that PRN use and adjustments to medications in general appear to be manageable and able to be executed with sufficient oversight and input from experts. As we will discuss next, these tiers of support and oversight are not nearly as established when considering when these protocols are warranted in a general education setting.

What Is the Impact on Students in General Education?

As it was mentioned in this and other chapters, students with disabilities are participating in the general education settings at unprecedented levels. In general education, the only mandates in place to govern the procedures discussed thus far are listed in the state's school code guidelines, in the school district's board policy, or are outlined in the district's student handbook. These guidelines should be considered the precedent and standard from which all decisions and accommodations are made. Any deviation away from these system-wide guidelines is typically accomplished through the IEP or 504 process and, as noted earlier, can be done when necessary.

The federal law, Individuals with Disabilities Education Act (IDEA) and more recent iteration of the Every Student Succeeds Act (ESSA), mandates that school entities look at the "least restrictive environment" (LRE) for students who qualify for special education services. We can go into a great discussion as to what the LRE is and is not, but this is an individual determination by the IEP team for each student. For the purpose of this chapter we are going to put LRE in laymen's terms, which can be considered the setting where a student can have the most access to his or her typical peers and exposure to the general education curriculum while still supporting his or her individual learning and, in this case, mental health needs sufficiently. Depending on the nature of a student's disability this can vary significantly. In the scenario posed at the beginning of this chapter, a student's IEP team will need to include plans and interventions to ensure safe and dignified access to medication when necessary and a plan for monitoring medicine use. For younger students, this will likely be a facilitated process where, due to the nature of the students, teachers and nurses will oversee administration, document changes, and report use to families, caregivers, and others in a rather straightforward manner. However, when we try to establish these procedures in general educational programs for older, more independent students, a multitude of challenging questions arise:

- What is the procedure to request to access medication for an older student or one who is more independent through the school day?

- Can the student come to the nurse's office or designated area to access medications? Once provided, does a student need to stay or can he or she go back to class?

- What if a family reports that their child has demonstrated independent, responsible use of medicines at home and wants this extended to the school setting?

- Can an IEP team allow a student to self-medicate? Can the IEP supersede a district's "no tolerance" policy for drugs?

- What steps need to be taken to be sure that other peers cannot access medications and ensure safety for all parties?

Beyond a plan of intervention for students themselves, school-wide teams also need to understand that policies and procedures are necessary to educate all staff members regarding safety around medications. At the most basic levels, staff and students should know what to do if a pill or bottle is found. Stakeholders also need to understand the procedures for supporting students who do have approved access to medicines (as documented through the IEP or Section 504 plan). This includes staff being acutely aware of the protocols for medication use. Policies should also outline the necessary documentation that needs to be carried out. Finally, policy language also needs to identify who will communicate this occurrence with caregivers and other relevant parties.

One final area to be considered should be the dignity of the affected student. Consider the precedents that would necessitate PRN medication use such as anxiety or panic attacks, explosive outbursts, overreactions, or even sensory sensitivities. These are not episodes with which a student is likely to want to engage. These are instead acute and traumatic reactions to their environment. Moreover, in these acute situations it should be assumed that students have lost the ability to regulate their bodies, their actions, and even their reactions when in crisis. Therefore, it is imperative that staff members make every attempt to protect and advocate for a student who is in this compromised state. This includes ensuring that the immediate environment is private and making sure the student is as comfortable as possible. It may additionally include communicating with caregivers or close friends of the student to limit the "mystique" or false assumptions surrounding the student or variables that resulted in the episode occurring. Finally, self-advocacy should be encouraged as well, where staff members are supporting the student to comfortably and assertively communicate with others about his or her strengths, needs, and why he or she requires the supports they do.

So, what can a medical professional do to maximize the effectiveness of his or her participation on these teams in alternative or public education settings? To coordinate logistics of medical intervention, nurses can volunteer to serve as a point person with outside medical or therapeutic service providers. To increase public awareness and accuracy in the information surrounding these interventions, nurses can function as a community-based service coordinator for families where, based on their expertise and relationship with medical providers, they can guide them to quality professionals and services. In their school teams, medical professionals can also provide professional development to fellow colleagues who may not be as versed in mental health diagnoses and medications. Finally, to maximize the quality and thoroughness of individualized plans, supplemental, medically focused plans can be drafted. While not federally or state mandated, medical professionals can guide the development of supplemental individualized health plans (IHPs) to outline daily health care needs. An extension of IHPs can also include an emergency care plan (ECPs), which can serve as another way to share protocols and procedures for medication use, ensuring dignity and safety (IRIS Center, n.d.).

Conclusion

Now more than ever students with more pervasive exceptionalities and challenging behaviors are included with typically developing peers or are attending alternative education programs. Regardless of the setting, professionals are bound to ensure safety, at minimum, and, optimally, promote authentic educational experience for these students, despite their differences. To make this a reality, the practice of supporting these students is outlined through federal mandates such as ADA, IDEA, and ESSA. Moreover, these accommodations are planned, monitored, and documented through the interdisciplinary activity of the IEP and Section 504 processes.

Medication use can be included as one of these supports, especially for students having cyclical mental health symptoms and severely challenging behaviors that compromise safety. When these medications are part of a student's plan of care, clear procedures and protocols need to be in place to ensure safe access for students and those around them. When medications are used, plans and procedures are also needed to provide consistency in administration, documentation, and follow up with relevant stakeholders in and outside the school setting. Throughout all these efforts, there is a fundamental need for effective communication and collaboration across all members of the student's IEP or 504 team to successfully accomplish these tasks. When supporting these students in alternative settings, the IEP team should be sure to include therapeutic and mental health professionals as well. Some students may even benefit from supplemental planning such as an IHP or ECP companion dedicated specifically to medication use and monitoring. It is crucial for student success and continued access to the least restrictive programming that teams maintain an effective focus on how supports, such as medications, are to be used to make progress toward overall educational goals.

References

Cardoso, A., & Xavier, M. (2015). Relationship between medication adherence and beliefs in patients with mental health disorders. *European Psychiatry, 30*(1), 232.

IRIS Center. (n.d.). School nurses: Roles and responsibilities in the school setting. Retrieved from https://iris.peabody.vanderbilt.edu/module/nur01-personnel/

Pennsylvania Department of Health. (2010, June 21). *Guidelines for Pennsylvania schools for the administration of medications and emergency care.* Retrieved from https://www.health.pa.gov/topics/Documents/School Health/Final Medication Manual.pdf

EXTENSION ACTIVITIES

Discussion Questions

1. The Pennsylvania Department of Health requires all schools where medications are being used to have a plan for administration, emergency care, and treatment. Would this type of plan support the student described in our scenario sufficiently? As it was noted in the original scenario, the student's mother delivered the medications and requested that they be used as needed from that point forward. What steps would need to be completed prior to usage of the medication throughout the school day?

    a. Discuss how you would deal with this as the special education teacher.

b. Discuss how you would solve this problem if you were a school administrator.

c. What role does the school nurse have in this scenario?

d. How will you ensure you are not putting one person's needs over another's?

e. Identify what laws you are abiding by or that are supporting your decisions.

2. How does a school district determine whether a student can access medications through the school day? How could individualized, special education planning be used to facilitate this process so that a student could maintain access to the least restrictive environment while having access to medications as a medically necessary support?

a. Explain how you would determine this if you were the one making the decision.

3. Could a case be made for changing a student's placement based on the frequency of medication utilization or the types of medications used? Explain your answer.

4. What if the intended behavioral effects are not observed when a student persists in demonstrating challenging behavior after medications are provided? What should be done? Explain your answer.

5. Research the use of psychotropic medications in schools for the student with mental health or developmental needs.

a. Do the benefits of having medication supports in schools outweigh the potential disadvantages? Explain your answer.

Write a Letter Assignment

Pick a side:

Write a letter from a parent's view to your child's school administrator outlining the reasons why your child should have access to PRN medications with him or her throughout the school day.

Write a letter from a parent's view opposing having a student using PRN medications in your child's classroom.

Discussion Paper

After reading this chapter, find a minimum of two additional articles that support this topic and write a double-spaced discussion paper following APA guidelines, including a bibliography page, to address the following:

- Before reading this chapter, my opinion on this issue was _____.

- In your own words, what is the issue at hand?

- Analyze what you see as the two sides of this issue.

- Identify a perceived misconception from either side. (When doing this, list the actual sentence(s) or portion of the sentence, citing the page number that you are referring to, then write your response as to why you think it is a misconception. The key word is "perceived.")

- And finally, which side do you personally agree with more and why? (Refer to your own experiences, here. If you have dealt with this issue in your personal life, work, teaching, etc., include that information in your answer.)

- Make sure to include in-text citations (when appropriate) from the supporting articles that you found.

Chapter 14

Mental Health Screenings
Should Schools be Responsible for Conducting Annual Student Screenings?

Toni L. Mild

PICTURE THIS: It's a typical Thursday afternoon and your school day is almost over. During your prep period at the end of the day, your cell phone alerts you that there has been a school shooting at a high school in a neighboring town. When you get home that evening, you sit down to dinner with your spouse, a fellow educator, and discuss this latest act of violence. The two of you are deeply troubled by this news due to the close vicinity of this recent tragedy. You begin to question what can be done differently so that shootings and acts of violence are not a common occurrence on the evening news. And more importantly, as educators, you want to ensure safety in your own organizations for not only yourself but also your students. In your discussion, you and your spouse discuss how there must be a mental health issue with the shooter, because people who are well adjusted and feeling good about themselves and others do not typically exhibit this type of extreme, violent behavior. Your spouse brings up whether schools should begin screening students for mental health conditions.

What Is the Issue?

Mental health is a term used to describe a person's thinking and behavior and is usually compared to what is considered acceptable within society. According to the American Psychiatric Association (as stated by National Council for Behavioral Health, 2016), "A … mental illness is a diagnosable illness that affects a person's thinking, emotional state, and behavior as well as disrupts the person's ability to work or carry out other daily activities and engage in satisfying personal relationships" (p. 4). The number of mental disorders diagnosed is growing each year. Studies indicate that almost 20% of the population are affected by some sort of mental illness. The onset of these disorders often manifests during the adolescent years.

It is very common for a person to schedule yearly check-ups with their physician in order to monitor their physical health. It is also common for a person to need follow-up care after this appointment. This may come in the form of filling a prescription, adjusting their diet, and so on. However, when we discuss mental health, there is a definite stigma that exists. People are not as open to discussing mental health issues with friends or colleagues the same way they are when talking about their need to change their diet or that their doctor just put them on a stanine to help lower their cholesterol. Why is taking care of one's body socially acceptable but taking care of one's mental health needs is considered a weakness?

Statistics show that around one out of five adults across the United States is estimated to have a mental health disorder and more than 20% of children at some point in their lives will also be diagnosed (National Council of Behavioral Health, 2016). If there is that much need for mental health assistance, why is society still not accepting? There is no single answer to this question, but we can gain some insight if we look at the history of mental health. Several decades ago, people who had mental health issues were hidden away in institutions or asylums. These individuals were viewed as scary and unstable. The public as a whole simply did not have the knowledge base and understanding to be accepting. Many derogatory names and terms were used, and unfortunately some are still in existence today.

Over the years, programs and resources have improved, but there is still a stigma about mental health. Many cities have a plethora of resources, but many rural communities have limited means to addressing the ongoing needs associated with mental illness. Some of these resources available aren't always appropriate or customized in a manner to meet the needs of all individuals. In addition, some of the workers in these organizations have such massive caseloads that they cannot meet the needs of all the clients and their families, which makes the turnover rate in this field quite high.

If adolescents are starting to show signs of mental illness during their teen years and are not getting diagnosed or receiving treatment, it is likely that the illness will continue to get worse throughout the years. Unfortunately, is it common to hear after a mass shooting that the perpetrator had suffered from some type of mental illness or had shown with his or her behavior that something was off. Many of the shootings across the country end with the offender either committing suicide or putting him- or herself in a situation for police-assisted suicide. According to the National Council of Behavioral Health (2016), suicide is the second leading cause of death for young people ages 10–24. Obviously not all teens who commit suicide go to the extreme of planning out and implementing a mass shooting, but society needs to intervene and assist these children before one more life is lost to suicide.

Ultimately, if the statistics previously mentioned are correct, there is a critical need for some sort of intervention in the field of mental health. If local and county resources are not meeting the need in their area, should schools be required to conduct screenings? After all, many schools conduct screenings for vision, hearing, body mass index (BMI), scoliosis, and so on. Would adding a screening for mental health issues really be that different from what they're already doing in these other areas?

What Does the Law Say?

To date, there are no laws that mandate schools conduct mental health screenings. Some schools across the United States have conducted mental health screenings of their students, but this has been done solely by choice, not mandate.

The Americans with Disabilities Act (ADA) does not mandate screenings; however, it does address equal opportunities for employment and for state and local government entities, public transportation, and so on for individuals with mental health and substance abuse needs.

The U.S. Department of Health and Human Services addresses the needs of individuals with substance abuse and mental health issues through the Substance Abuse and Mental Health Services Administration (SAMHSA). Although there are no regulations in place for school districts to provide screenings, SAMHSA does attempt to assist in the regulation of insurance coverage and cost for services required to treat individuals with mental health and substance abuse needs through the Affordable Care Act of 2010. SAMHSA also assists in improving the type of care provided for children and adolescents with mental health and substance abuse needs through the Children's Health Act of 2000 (Substance Abuse and Mental Health Services Administration, 2018).

How Does This Affect Schools?

Schools are deeply affected when students have mental health needs. If the need is undiagnosed, it is common for there to be signs that are visible throughout the school day, usually seen through the student's behavior. The behavior can be apparent such as in the case of a student who becomes volatile. Those behaviors are usually addressed sooner due to their aggressive and intense nature. On the other hand, some students may show shy, introverted, or withdrawn behaviors. These students usually do not get identified as early due to them not necessarily showing extreme behaviors that interfere with classroom instruction. These students can hide in the back of the class, never causing problems for the teacher.

Due to the onset of mental health issues being common during the adolescent years, how does a school determine whether the behavior being exhibited is part of normal adolescent development or is a sign of a true mental health illness? Normal adolescent development includes many changes. These changes can be physical, mental, or social. It is very common during puberty to experience changes in all of these areas. Teens often become moody for no apparent reason, can become confrontational if someone disagrees with their viewpoint, and can also show impulsive behaviors in which their decision making is not always well planned or thought out. Physically there are changes to the body—weight loss, weight gain, acne, and hair growth, just to name a few. Socially, it is common for adolescents to take on new friend groups, become a part of new activities, and find new interests.

It is not an easy task to determine whether many of the changes experienced during adolescence are part of normal adolescent development or whether they should be viewed as red flags. One thing that educators can do to monitor students is to get to know them, their likes, and interests. If an educator sees major changes occurring, that could represent an issue in terms of needing help. This is especially true if they know a student to be a big fan of a particular group or activity and then he or she suddenly stops that activity and doesn't replace it with anything. It is common for interests to change, but those interests are usually replaced with something else. This is just one example of what schools can look for, but there are many other areas that need to be addressed and identified. Is there an effective tool that a school can utilize that could provide valid, reliable information about a student's mental health that the school can share with the parent or guardian?

What Is the Impact on Students Needing Special Education or 504 Plan Services?

Special education is one area in the school setting that can and does identify students with severe mental health issues. Under the Individuals with Disabilities Education Act (IDEA) and Pennsylvania's Chapter 14 regulations, students who exhibit severe emotional disturbance display behaviors, over a long period of time, that negatively affect their educational performance. Many students with severe emotional disturbance will receive specially designed instruction and supplemental aids and services outlined in an individualized education program (IEP) that may also contain a behavior intervention plan (BIP), which outlines specific goals and objectives for the student to work on over the course of the school year. The BIP will outline specific procedures for all teachers and staff who are working with the child to adhere to based on the student's behavior(s) of concern.

The IEP is reviewed annually, and any new programming needs or services can be added or removed based on the progress or lack of progress the student has made. The student is also re-evaluated by the school psychologist at a minimum of every 3 years. Any new findings will be communicated to the IEP team through the evaluation report and spelled out more thoroughly in the IEP and BIP.

Students who do not qualify for services under IDEA or Chapter 14 provisions may be eligible for services under the American's with Disabilities Act (ADA) or Chapter 15/504. The ADA mandates equal opportunities for persons with mental health or substance abuse needs. Schools can implement a Chapter 15/504 plan that outlines what accommodations would be made for a particular student throughout the school day in order to have the same opportunities as other students. The plan could give the student opportunities to meet with the school counselor, check in with the school nurse (for medication monitoring), or utilize a support animal. These are just a few of the many types of accommodations that may be found on this type of 504 plan.

What Is the Impact on Students in General Education?

Students in the general education setting would also be impacted by this initiative. Screenings would be conducted for *all* students, not just ones receiving special education or in need of a 504 plan. According to the statistics, it is likely that the majority of students with a mental illness would be in the general education setting and have not been identified. The general education population would be the most affected by a school-wide screening.

In order for a school-wide screening to take place, there would need to be administrative and school board buy in and support. The district would need to create a board policy outlining this screening, including the procedures, grade levels, and parental communication of results following the screening. Districts would also need to conduct extensive research to identify a screening tool that will give them valid, reliable results. They would also need to determine what the next steps would be if a student scored within the at-risk range. Creating partnerships with mental health care providers in the community would also be of great benefit. It would cause problems to begin identifying mental health issues in the school when there are no or limited resources to turn to for assistance.

When schools conduct vision screenings, if a student shows signs of poor vision, the parent is contacted and asked to follow up with an optometrist. It is then up to the parent whether they follow through with this suggestion. Due to mental health being a controversial topic, it would be a good idea for districts to ask for parent permission to conduct the screening. Although this is not done for the other screenings that schools do, it would be in their best interest to gain parental support, especially if this is a new initiative in that district. The school would also need to outline procedures after an at-risk communication has been sent home to parents. They would also need to provide a list of providers for parents or guardians to contact for assistance and treatment.

Conclusion

In summary, mental illness is a growing issue with teens and young adults across the country today. Each year the number of Americans diagnosed with a mental disorder continues to climb. With the average onset age for these disorders being the teenage years, schools need to be educated on what is normal adolescent behavior versus what are warning signs of a mental illness.

With this growing need, schools will need to determine if providing a screening for mental illness is something they wish to tackle. There are numerous ways districts could provide this service—mandated, optional, or parent or teacher referral. And likely, what works for one district will not work for another. It will need to be a decision each district makes based on community support, need, and availability of community mental health providers and resources. No matter what decision a district makes, just starting the conversation is one step toward reducing the stigma associated with mental health and mental illness.

References

American Psychiatric Association (APA). (2000). Diagnostic and statistical manual of mental disorders (4th ed.) (SDM-IV-TR). Washington, DC: Author.

National Council for Behavioral Health. (2016). *Mental health first aid USA: For adults assisting young people.* Washington, DC.

Substance Abuse and Mental Health Services Administration. (2018). *Laws and regulations.* Retrieved from https://www.samhsa.gov/about-us/who-we-are/laws-regulations

EXTENSION ACTIVITIES

Discussion Questions

1. You are a school board member and your district just decided to mandate mental health screenings for all students. You are currently a part of the policy team and are drafting the procedures for what to do when the results for a student come back as at risk. What procedures will you put into place?
   a. Discuss with whom this information would be shared.
   b. What will the parent or guardian information contain?
   c. Are there any follow-up requirements by district staff or parents?

2. As a young adult, you have dealt with depression off and on for many years. You have some strong opinions on identification and the type of treatments used. One of your students has confided in you about his depression but states that his parents refuse to seek treatment for him and just tell him, "That's life; suck it up." What will you do in this situation in terms of interactions with
   a. the student,
   b. the student's parents, and
   c. other staff within your school district?

3. You are a second-year teacher and are finding that you are in over your head in terms of how to deal with some of the behaviors you are seeing in your classes. Some students are belligerent and rude, others are shy and you can't get two words out of them, and yet others are doing well in your

class and seem to have tons of friends but you are overhearing that the activities they are engaging in outside of school are dangerous.

    a. What can you do to improve on your overall knowledge base and management of students in your classroom?

    b. What types of professional development opportunities would you register for?

    c. Is there anything that administration could do to support you and the rest of the teachers in this area?

4. Discuss whose responsibility it is to diagnose mental health issues.

    a. Are schools overstepping their bounds if they mandate a school-wide screening?

    b. Is it a service that schools should be required to provide to parents as part of a student's educational, physical, and social well-being?

    c. Is this issue private and one that schools have no right interfering in?

5. If a child is found to be at risk or as having a mental health issue, what should be done?

    a. Can a school mandate that treatment be sought?

    b. Can parents decide to do nothing?

    c. What if the student doesn't want help or treatment? Does he or she have a say?

Write a Letter Assignment

Pick a side:

You are a teacher. Write a letter to your superintendent/school board in favor of school-wide mental health screening. Include specific reasons as to why it is needed and what it could look like in your school district.

Write a letter from a parent's view to your school's superintendent/school board opposing the use of school-wide mandated mental health screening. Outline the reasons why your child should not be required to be a part of this screening and how this infringes on your rights as a parent/guardian.

Discussion Paper

After reading this chapter, find a minimum of two additional articles that support this topic and write a double-spaced discussion paper following APA guidelines, including a bibliography page, to address the following:

- Before reading this chapter, my opinion on this issue was _____.

- In your own words, what is the issue at hand?

- Analyze what you see as the two sides of this issue.

- Identify a perceived misconception from either side. (When doing this, list the actual sentence(s) or portion of the sentence, citing the page number that you are making reference to, then write your response as to why you think it is a misconception. The key word is "perceived.")

- And finally, which side do you personally agree with more and why? (Refer to your personal experiences, here. If you have dealt with this issue in your personal life, work, teaching, etc., include that information in your answer.)

- Make sure to include in-text citations (when appropriate) from the supporting articles that you found.

Section VIII

School Leadership

Chapter 15

Administrator Preparation
Are Certification Programs Preparing Public School
Principals to Lead Special Education?

Amanda J. Truitt-Smith

PICTURE THIS: A fully included 10th-grade special education student meets all IEP objectives for 5 consecutive years. The student has been making progress in the general education curriculum with modifications and support. The student's placement on the IEP indicates an itinerant level for both learning support and speech-language support services; the student receives a resource/study hall period for 42 minutes per day and one 30-minute speech-language session per week. At the student's 3-year re-evaluation, language testing indicated language skills to be within average parameters for all areas tested. Based on progress in the general education curriculum, achievement of IEP goals over consecutive years, and performance on the assessments given, speech-language services were discharged. Following the RR meeting, the student's parents were not happy with a score within the average range on a standardized assessment; they reported it was the responsibility of the district's special education department to ensure the student was pushed to be above average. At a follow-up conference between the high school principal and the parents, the principal agreed with the parents, stating, "The special education department had set the bar too low." The high school principal then proceeded to inform the staff, "It's my professional opinion that we move forward and raise the bar for student X and discuss new ways to move him from average to a new level."

What Is the Issue?

For more than 35 years, special education has been a much-discussed topic in the education world. "Resulting from landmark social and legislative events, special education in the United States has undergone drastic changes over the past 30 years" (Lynch, 2012, p. 44). The Education for All Handicapped Children Act, (public law (PL) 94–142) passed by Congress in 1975 (Individuals with Disabilities Education Act (IDEA), 2004), set the wheels in motion for decades-long debates and reviews of practices relating to special education.

After multiple amendments, the Individuals with Disabilities Education Act (IDEA) (PL 108–446), was established to protect the rights of students with disabilities and guaranteed them the right to a free and appropriate public education (FAPE) (Bateman & Bateman, 2001; IDEA, 2004; Wright & Wright, 2007; Yell, 2004). The impact of special education reform has been felt from administration all the way to the classroom. The connection of "special education administration with the educational leadership curriculum is at once a current problem and a perennial concern" (Crockett, 2002, p. 158) for public school principals throughout the nation. Public school principals have a critical role in the development of special education programming, curriculum planning, professional development for teachers under their supervision, and evaluating the fidelity of current programs in place (Crockett, 2002; Cruzeiro & Morgan, 2006). It is crucial public school principals be well versed in special education content knowledge and procedures to ensure their school adheres to the law and operates smoothly.

Several studies have been conducted across the country researching public school principals and their knowledge of special education content, all of which suggest increased training in special education is warranted. It is imperative public school principals are knowledgeable in this critical area. Further review of the research is needed to identify the special education knowledge, skill set, and beliefs held by public school principals; this information is vital to certify public school principals are provided the appropriate pre-certification coursework and learning experiences. Research is warranted to ensure the public school principal has knowledge of special education law, policies, and procedures to diminish litigation opportunities. The public school principal must take a hard look at his or her own practices to determine if he or she is providing high-quality education to students who receive special education supports and services that are allowing them to reach their full potential.

The research has demonstrated that, overall, public school principals receive little to no formal training in leading special education in their degree and/or certification programs (Angelle & Bilton, 2009, Wakeman, Browder, Flowers, & Ahlgrim-Delzell, 2006). This inadequacy of leadership is due mostly to a lack of the public school principals' unfamiliarity with the unique aspects and key features of special education, a lack of technical competence for special education terminology, eligibility requirements, student learning outcomes, and knowledge regarding their specific leadership role as it pertains to special education laws, policies, and procedures. There is no standard for coursework in certification programs, nor are there educational prerequisites when it comes to special education content in principal certification programs. The physical education teacher receives the same training as the special education teacher; both capable candidates, yet one requires extensive teaching and hands-on learning to acquire knowledge of special education laws and procedures while the other requires minimal guidance.

These factors contribute to the diminished public school principal's leadership role in the day-to-day operations that surround special education programming. Special education leadership should be a significant concern for public school principals as their roles have increased due to ensuring successful outcomes for all students, the increased number of students placed in special education programs, the high cost associated with educating students in special education, and the due process ramifications if educational outcomes are not achieved (Angelle & Bilton, 2009; Davis, 1980).

What Does the Law Say?

Today thousands of students throughout the nation receive special education services and supports due to the passage of landmark legislation known as public law 94–142, the Education for All Handicapped Children Act of 1975 (Bateman & Bateman, 2001; Wright & Wright, 2007; Yell, 2004). Prior to the passage of PL 94–142, school-aged students with disabilities were typically excluded from public schools. In 1990, PL–142 was amended, and along with those changes came the first version of IDEA. Since its initial passage, IDEA has been amended and now includes transition services and safeguards for parents. IDEA was most recently reauthorized in 2004 with two primary purposes. The first purpose was to provide an education that meets a special education student's unique needs and prepare the student for further education, employment, and independent living. IDEA's second purpose was to protect the rights of both special education students and their parents. Public school principals must have a solid understanding of IDEA to ensure best practices are being adhered to when the IEP is implemented.

IDEA is based on six major principles: zero reject, non-discriminatory identification and evaluation, FAPE, least restrictive environment (LRE), due process safeguards, and parent involved decision making. Zero reject dictates that public schools must educate all students with disabilities regardless of the nature or severity of the disability. Public school districts are required to provide educational programming to students aged 3–21 (Heward, 2000; IDEA, 2004; Wright & Wright, 2007; Yell, 2004). Under IDEA, public school districts must use unbiased evaluation methods to determine special education eligibility. Evaluations must not rely on one test measure to make the determination if a student is eligible for services; this includes testing a student in his or her native language. Principles three and four guarantee all public school students have access to FAPE in the LRE. FAPE and LRE must be provided to students at no cost to the parent.

It is imperative public school principals demonstrate a thorough understanding of IEP creation and implementation; additionally, principals must be active participants in the identification process "to ensure not only that the district follows appropriate procedures, but that the student receives an appropriate education" (Bateman & Bateman, 2001, p. 12). Too often principals become involved in the special education process when funding decisions need to be made, such as paraprofessional support services or student placement in an alternative setting. Public school principals should remain apprised of current educational programming and the needs of the special education students in their district; they must remain aware of what has been successful in the past and what supports and encourages student achievement. By keeping abreast of students within their walls, public school principals can make efficient informed decisions, be aware of a student's educational needs, prevent delays in programming, and sanction adequate resources and support services.

The LRE clause mandates special education is a continuum of services; students should only be removed from the general education classroom setting when supplementary aides and services cannot provide them a meaningful education. The IEP must address and justify why a student is not in the general education classroom setting. IDEA also safeguards the rights of students and their families. Parental consent must be received for all evaluations and placement determinations. Lastly, IDEA provides provisions for parent and student input when making decisions for students receiving special education services (Bateman & Bateman, 2001; Heward, 2000; IDEA, 2004; Katsiyannis, Losinski, & Prince, 2012; Wright & Wright, 2007; Yell, 2004).

Public school principals must have a working knowledge of the foundations of special education so that they can ensure resources are allocated appropriately (Bateman & Bateman, 2001). Take for example the case mentioned in the opening scenario: The principal was unaware of eligibility criteria for special education placement of a related service. Due to the principal's lack of special education knowledge, unnecessary hours were spent re-evaluating the student, meeting with the parent, educating the principal on eligibility guidelines, and completing paperwork. Principals are there to support all, staff included; had the aforementioned principal had a thorough understanding of special education eligibility guidelines prior to making grandiose statements, the principal would not have orchestrated a discord and divide between the school and the family, created resentment among staff, nor called into question the competency of those involved in the decision to discharge services. Public school principal certification programs must do a better job at educating school leaders in their coursework; one or two special education classes is insufficient. Special education should become a competency for future public school leaders.

How Does This Affect Schools?

As mentioned previously, special education students and their families have their rights to FAPE in the LRE, guaranteed under the law, thanks in part to the procedural safeguards of IDEA (Bateman & Bateman, 2001; Heward, 2000; IDEA, 2004; Wright & Wright, 2007; Yell, 2004). Most IDEA litigation due process cases are due to violations of FAPE, tuition reimbursement, and compensatory education (Zirkel, 2012). Due process rights are protected via legislation to ensure that, in the event there is disagreement between the school district and the parents, either party can initiate a due process. Special education litigation costs school districts millions of dollars and has an adverse effect on the relationships between the home and school (Mueller, 2009; Wright & Wright, 2007; Yell, 2004). Public school principals "need to know the rights and obligations of the parents and the district, the process, how to prepare for a hearing, what is involved, the principal's role, and what happens when the hearing is over" (Bateman & Bateman, 2001, p. 103). It is critical the public school principal be informed; knowledge is power. When dealing with special education, public school principals must ensure their staff are adhering to the law, complying with IEPs, utilizing available resources, and involving families; if these conditions are met, there is reduced room for error and due process proceedings.

Due process hearings are "to resolve differences of opinion between parents and school officials regarding the education, placement, or services for the child with a disability" (Bateman & Bateman, 2001, p. 16). The first landmark due process case to reach the Supreme Court after the establishment of PL 94–142 was brought via an appeal by a school district regarding the special education services of first grader, Amy Rowley. In the *Board of Education of Hendrick Hudson Central School District v. Rowley* (1982), the lower courts ruled the school district was required to pay for a sign language interpreter for a student with hearing impairment, Amy, to enable her access to FAPE in the curriculum (Bateman & Bateman, 2001; Sage & Burrello, 1994; Wright & Wright, 2007; Yell, 2004). The "Supreme Court concluded FAPE has two prongs, the first being procedural compliance, and the second being a relatively relaxed substantive standard" (Zirkel, 2016, p. 1); this became known as the Rowley standard.

The Rowley standard is a two-prong test used by courts to determine whether public school districts have provided FAPE as mandated under IDEA. The first prong of the Rowley standard is deciding if the school has complied with the procedures of IDEA (Wright & Wright, 2007; Yell, 2004; Zirkel, 2016). The second part determines whether the IEP, which is to be based on the principles of IDEA, is detailed so students receive educational benefit(s) from their placement and goals (Wright & Wright, 2007; Yell, 2004; Zirkel, 2016). The decision from the Rowley case remains relevant and important when a court is deciding whether a student is receiving FAPE. Public school principals need an understanding of historical court decisions such as Rowley; knowing how special education has evolved legally can help prevent districts from making costly mistakes that result in litigation. When it comes to special education topics, it is the duty of the public school principal to ensure history does not repeat itself. This author questions whether principals with less than 5 years' experience could define the Rowley standard or identify landmark court decisions of the past.

FAPE has been the reason many cases have made it to the Supreme Court. The landmark cases of *Irving Independent School District v. Tatro* (468 U.S. 883) (1984), *School Committee of Town of Burlington, Mass. v. Department of Educ. of Mass.* (471 U.S. 359) (1985), *Honig v. Doe* (484 U.S. 305) (1988), and *Florence County School Dist. Four v. Carter* (510 U.S. 7) (1993) all address FAPE violations to some degree (Heward, 2000; Wright & Wright, 2007; Yell, 2004; Zirkel, 2016). Zirkel (2013) completed a review of 224 court decisions to look for trends in special education cases. Out of the cases reviewed, states with the highest FAPE violations were "(1) New York—thirty-five (16%); (2) California—thirty-two (14%); (3) Hawaii—twenty-two (10%); (4) Pennsylvania—nineteen (8%); (5) New Jersey—thirteen (6%); (6) Texas—eleven (5%); and (7) Alaska—ten (4%)" (Zirkel, 2013, p. 226). It is imperative public school districts strive to follow IDEA regulations to reduce litigation statistics; public school principals who know the history of the law can avoid costly mistakes. Public school principal certification programs require courses on school law, not special education law. Competency in special education law should be mandatory.

The Supreme Court's latest decision regarding FAPE was in *Endrew F. v. Douglas County School District RE-1. Endrew* addressed the substantive standard for the central obligation of FAPE under IDEA. The "Court had not revisited this issue for 35 years, having originally addressed it in its landmark IDEA decision in the *Board of Education of Hendrick Hudson Central School District v. Rowley*" (Zirkel, 2017, p. 1). In a unanimous decision in March 2017, the U.S. Supreme Court ruled in favor of a higher standard for students with disabilities. Endrew F.'s case revolved around one main theme: "Must schools provide a meaningful education in which children show significant progress and are given substantially equal opportunities as typical children, or can they provide an education that results in just some improvement" (Mackenna, 2017, para. 4). The *Endrew F.* decision highlighted the fact the IEP process is team based and should include opinions of professionals *and* parents; the IEP team should collectively work together for the betterment of the student. The IEP team must also include the public school principal; a principal who remains ignorant of students' needs in their district cannot adequately advocate for their education.

Definitions of identification categories have changed over the years, and some states have adopted alternative frameworks, yet the notion of identifying and categorizing primary disabilities remains an element of the law (Bateman & Bateman, 200; IDEA, 2004; Wright & Wright, 2007; Yell, 2004). Under IDEA in 2018, 12 disability categories exist; public-school principals must have a working knowledge of the disability labels, entry criteria, and supports available to ensure their students are working to reach their full potential. A fundamental goal of education is to equip all students with the knowledge, skills, and tools necessary to think critically, solve problems, and succeed when they exit formalized schooling. Public school principals are tasked with ensuring all students are held to the same standard of learning and must be knowledgeable in special education to provide success (Bays & Crockett, 2007; Wakeman et al., 2006).

Ethical dilemmas arise frequently in the field of special education. In the public school system, students in special education are considered the minority; they make up a small percentage of the collective (Billingsley, 2004; Bon & Bigbee, 2011). As a minority, their best interests and rights are protected under IDEA; this protection should be supported by each public school district's principal. Often when public school principals make decisions that affect students with disabilities, there is a distinction made between the best interests of the individual student versus the student population. Public school principals think "about the best interests of students in general, as a corporate body, and when specific student-related issues c[ome] to their attention they alter their perspectives on students' best interest and focus on unique, individual student needs" (Frick & Faircloth, 2007, p. 30). IDEA and No Child Left Behind (NCLB) dictate what public school principals can do when it comes to students in special education. Public school principals must pay attention to how current and future school policies and initiatives may affect public school principals' abilities to respond to individual needs while creating a learning environment for all.

What Is the Impact on Students Needing Special Education or 504 Plan Services?

Public school principals are expected to be instructional leaders for all students in their district (National Policy Board for Educational Administration (NPBEA), 2015). When it comes to leadership for students with disabilities, many public school principals lack experience in the field of special education and have limited pre-service training in special education–related issues. In the case of the physical education teacher versus the special education teacher, which individual is going to feel more comfortable being the LEA at an IEP? As mandated by law, public schools have the responsibility to identify students with learning and behavior deficits to enable them to receive supports to achieve academic success (Hallahan, Kauffman, & Pullen, 2015; IDEA, 2004; Wright & Wright, 2007; Yell, 2004). The 2004 reauthorization of IDEA reaffirmed the notion that students in special education had the right to be educated in the general education classroom setting with their non-exceptional peers (IDEA, 2004; Wright & Wright, 2007; Yell, 2004). Public school principals must feel comfortable taking the lead when it comes to special education. The public school principal oversees the building; thus, all decisions made reflect on their leadership abilities. The public school principal must be able to make informed special education decisions as they may be required to be the overseer of the special education department and frequently act as the LEA.

Special education leadership should be a significant concern for school public school principals; "to establish cultures that support the development of all students, certain attitudinal, organizational, and instructional changes must occur" (Ball & Green, 2005, p. 57). Special education leadership should be at the forefront for public school principals. Public school principal preparation programs must adapt their programs to prepare future principals to meet the demands of special education to successfully lead all schools. Once a principal receives a leadership position, there is no time for mentoring; they have become the mentor. Possessing a basic competency in special education prior to entering the field should be mandatory.

Principal preparation and certification programs do not provide enough background knowledge in special education to adequately prepare public school administrators for the rigors of special education programming (Bargerhuff, 2001; Christensen, Robertson, Williamson, & Hunter, 2010; Frost & Kerston, 2009). NCLB mandated all public schools be accountable for the academic success of all students as measured by adequate yearly progress (AYP), including students with disabilities. NCLB supported the inclusion of students in special education programs in the general education curriculum. Inclusion is defined as "providing all students, including those with significant disabilities, equitable opportunities to receive effective educational services, with the needed supplementary aids and supports services, in age appropriate schools, in their neighborhood schools" (Bargerhuff, 2001, p. 2).

NCLB further strengthened the mandates of IDEA as the focus was on the inclusion of all students in a district, as well as special education student participation in state and federal testing (Bargerhuff, 2001; NCLB, 2002; Voltz & Collins, 2010; Wright & Wright, 2007; Yell, 2004). NCLB targeted students with disabilities, students with limited English proficiency, students with minority status, and those with an economic disadvantage.

Inclusion is an essential component of IDEA and protects the rights of students with disabilities. From 1990 to 2007, student placement among 6- to 17-year-old students with high incidence disabilities placed in separate settings or schools decreased by 25%; placement using the pullout service delivery model decreased by 30%; and placement in general education for students in special education increased by 93% (McLeskey, Landers, Williamson, & Hoppey, 2010). When talking about inclusion, public school principals must look at IDEA. IDEA has two key factors when thinking about the least restrictive environment. First, IDEA mandates students should be with their peers in general education to the maximum extent appropriate (Bargerhuff, 2001; McLeskey et al., 2010; NCLB, 2002; Voltz & Collins, 2010; Wright & Wright, 2007; Yell, 2004). Secondly, special classes, separate schools, or removal from the general education class should only happen when the disability is severe enough that supplementary aids and services can't provide an appropriate education. Carpenter (2008) writes inclusion is not that every "student is educated with peers at all times, but it does mean that the responsibility of discovering effective means for all students to learn together is taken very seriously, and deviations from this approach are made with reluctance and only after careful deliberation" (para. 4).

Principal beliefs and previous special education experience can influence current views regarding inclusion in the public school setting (Bargerhuff, 2001). Public school principals have a "critical role in the implementation of successful inclusion in diverse, standards-based environments" (Voltz & Collins, 2010, p. 70). Identified themes and benefits regarding inclusion models have been cited as "being with typical peers, exposure to everything and high expectations, individualized curricular and instructional supports, skilled and knowledgeable staff, collaboration and teaming, a positive and caring environment, and providing a balanced educational program" (Downing & Peckham-Hardin, 2007, p. 22). Other benefits for inclusion include increased awareness and tolerance of exceptionalities, increased empathy toward students with disabilities, learning while helping, and learning special skills (Bargerhuff, 2001; Downing & Peckham-Hardin, 2007; Voltz & Collins, 2010). A principal who believes inclusion is keeping special education students in the general education classroom with a paraprofessional at their side needs to revisit their textbooks, specifically reading chapters on inclusion and co-teaching.

The attitudes of public school principals "are important for inclusive practices, but not as important as the training and experience of the school leaders charged with implementing these practices" (Ball & Green, 2005, p. 72). Public school principals who had a prior background in special education viewed themselves as having more awareness and involvement in the special education department in their building. Principals must use the relational leadership style and provide staff the proper resources if inclusion is to be successful. For inclusion to be successful there must be continuous communication between regular and special education staff and support personnel (Bargerhuff, 2001). One of the core objectives for educator preparation programs "is the development of teachers capable of providing individually designed instruction that is reasonably calculated to provide educational benefit to eligible students with disabilities" (Crockett, 2002, p. 161); principal education programs should be no different. The main goal of special education is "finding and capitalizing on exceptional students' abilities" (Hallahan & Kauffman, 2015, p. 13). Pre-service certification programs must educate future public school leaders on inclusive practices (Bargerhuff, 2001; Crockett, 2002). If certification programs are not going to provide training, public school principals must self-educate on inclusive practices.

Principals have been recognized as vital contributors to the effectiveness of public schools. Every public school principal must have the proper knowledge, skill set, and frame of mind to be an effective school leader for all students. Principals must have working knowledge of all aspects of a school, including day-to-day operations that including curriculum, staffing, maintenance, and building/grounds (Bargerhuff, 2001; Frost & Kerston, 2009; Tubbs, Heard, & Epps, 2011; Voltz & Collins, 2010). Principal preparation and certification programs do not provide enough background knowledge in special education to adequately prepare public school principals for the rigors of special education programming (Bargerhuff, 2001; Christensen et al., 2010; Frost & Kerston, 2009; Tubbs, Heard, & Epps, 2011; Wakeman et. al, 2006). Public school principals need to actively seek ways to boost the achievement of the entire school population. Public school principals need to take a hard look at inclusion and use the LRE as a best practice guideline when making decisions for the entire school population.

What Is the Impact on Students in General Education?

Principals in public education are responsible for not only school leadership, but they are also accountable for referral and service delivery of special education programs in their school system (Crockett, 2002; Cruzeiro & Morgan, 2006; DiPaola, Tschannen-Moran, & Walther-Thomas, 2004). Lynch (2012) noted in the traditional role that "the principal assumed responsibility for general education students and the director of special education assumed responsibility for students with disabilities" (p. 42). Public school principals are required to not only be instructional leaders, but they are also responsible for special education programming, personnel issues, public relations, budgeting, curriculum, and ensuring students are making adequate yearly progress. On average 79% of a principal's time was spent on regular education and 21% was spent on special education issues (Cruzeiro & Morgan, 2006).

Public school principals have multiple duties and may choose to delegate responsibilities, yet they are still responsible for overall school management and program implementation for all. "Resulting from landmark social and legislative events, special education in the United States has undergone drastic changes over the past 30 years" (Lynch, 2012, p. 44). Principals are often involved in compliance and legal issues related to special education. According to the data, most interactions between principals and special education teachers revolved around paperwork and compliance; these interactions "may be necessary, but they are not sufficient to ensure positive learning outcomes for special education" (Bays & Crockett, 2007, p. 157). Public school principals should seek an instructional vision that identifies increased outcomes and performance for all, including special education staff; these outcomes could be offered via professional development to enhance collaboration, provide ongoing support and encouragement, and continually evaluate instruction of their teachers (Bays & Crockett, 2007; DiPaola, Tschannen-Moran, & Walther-Thomas, 2004; Frost & Kersten, 2011).

To face the many educational tasks and demands of the future, public school principals must cultivate "skills and strategies that are critical for providing a positive learning environment for a highly diverse student population" (Miller & Martin, 2014, p. 129). Competent public school principals should allocate time for "structuring the story of special education, ensuring that school practices on behalf of students with disabilities are grounded in the field's conceptual core" (Crockett, 2002, p. 160). Leadership should merge with data; data must drive decisions principals make daily. Principals must recognize and develop leadership skills of their current staff (Crockett, 2002; Crum, Sherman, & Myran, 2010). School accountability and conversations must be the front runner of all activities involving leadership. Due the importance of data-based decision making, it is critical leaders obtain multiple data sets from staff to make decisions. Public school principals must engulf themselves in their district to learn all they can about all aspects of the students they serve. Principals must have a working knowledge of IEP modifications and specially designed instruction and supports that are available; if data drives instructional decisions, the principal must be aware of said data.

The public school principal has multiple duties; DiPaola, Tschannen-Moran, and Walther-Thomas (2004) identified two critical areas that must receive leadership attention and support. To be an effective leader, public school principals should focus on improving professional skills and knowledge of the faculty and staff they lead and support (Crockett, 2002; DiPaola, Tschannen-Moran, &Walther-Thomas, 2004). The U.S. Department of Education and current public school principals need to look at developing special education–related areas as part of principal preparation and induction programs. Principals must be the instructional leader for their building. When hiring new staff, school boards should consider a candidate's background knowledge/resume and how much the potential school leader understands special education.

Public school principal education programs are not adequately preparing participants to be instructional leaders for special education (Lasky & Karge, 2006; Lynch, 2012; McHatton, Boyer, Shaunessy, & Terry, 2010; Pazey & Cole, 2013). Today's public school principals "must not only manage school finances, keep buses running on time, and make hiring decisions, but they must also be instructional leaders, data analysts, community relations officers, and change agents" (Interstate School Leaders Licensure Consortium Standards [ISLCC], 2008, p. 3). To special education leaders, public school principals require training on special education law, procedure, programs, and students with disabilities (Garrison-Wade, Sobel, & Fulmer, 2007; Wakeman et al., 2006). Wakeman, Browder, Flowers, and Ahlgrim-Delzell (2006) conducted a survey that revealed 92% of participating principals had no formal training in special education or a special education teaching certification or license. Angelle and Bilton (2009), Davis (1980), Lasky and Karge (2006), Lynch (2012), McHatton, Boyer, Shaunessy, and Terry (2013), and Pazey and Cole (2013) have all noted the discrepancy between principal preparation programs and subsequent practice. A survey conducted by Davis (1980) discovered most principals (51.9%) had never taken a special education class and only 32.8% had any prior exposure of special education students in their certification programs and training. A similar study conducted 26 years later revealed 36% of public school principals had no experience with special education in their training programs (Lasky & Karge, 2006), again raising the argument, what are certification programs doing to ensure the gym teacher is as knowledgeable as the special education certificate holder?

Special education competency and knowledge of special education law has been targeted as a critical skill for public school leaders; however, "within the context of social justice and school leadership, it is all but ignored" (Pazey & Cole, 2013, p. 249). A review of empirical literature indicated public school principals should receive training in 12 fundamental areas (Pazey & Cole, 2013). Those areas include communication and relationships (DiPaola & Tschannen-Moran, 2003; Taylor-Backor & Gordon, 2015; Pazey & Cole, 2003), leadership and vision (Darling-Hammond, LaPointe, Meyerson, Orr, & Cohen, 2007; DiPaola, Tschannen-Moran, & Walther-Thomas, 2004; Pazey & Cole, 2013), budget (Pazey & Cole, 2003), special education (Angelle & Bilton, 2009; Bateman & Bateman, 2001; McHatton et al., 2010; Pazey & Cole, 2013), curriculum and instruction, personnel, data analysis, collaboration (DiPaola, Tschannen-Moran, & Walther-Thomas, 2004; Pazey & Cole, 2013), special education programs (Lasky & Karge, 2006; Lynch, 2012; Pazey & Cole, 2013), professional development (Darling-Hammond et al., 2007; Taylor-Backor & Gordon, 2015), the organization (Darling-Hammond et al., 2007; Pazey & Cole, 2013), and advocacy (Darling-Hammond et al., 2007; Pazey & Cole, 2013).

Although special education was listed as one of the identified competencies for public-school principals, it continues to be ignored in certification programs (DiPaola, Tschannen-Moran, &Walther-Thomas, 2004; Lasky & Karge, 2006; Lynch, 2012; Pazey & Cole, 2013). Lynch (2012) reported that "a review of state certification requirements indicated that only eight states required special education training for pre-service principals" (p. 45). To be an effective leader, it is essential public school principals be informed of the evidence-based practices that engulf regular and special education (Angelle & Bilton, 2009; DiPaola, Tschannen-Moran, & Walther-Thomas, 2004; McHatton et al., 2010; Pazey & Cole, 2013). To do so, public school principals should receive training in special education areas beyond learning the defining characteristics of a disability; school leaders must have a solid grasp of IDEA, procedural safeguard, due process, zero reject, discipline, the IEP process, and state-mandated reports (Angelle & Bilton, 2009; Bateman & Bateman, 2001; McHatton et al., 2010; Pazey & Cole, 2013). Special education law and procedures must be an integral part of certification programs.

Public school principal preparation programs must be "designed to meet the challenges of school improvement, not just graduate certified managers who lack the depth to lead effective school change" (Reames, 2010, p. 440). Special education needs to be considered and discussed as much as gender, class, and race; it is time to make special education part of the discussion, not the afterthought (Frost & Kersten, 2011). A public school principal who does not receive special education training in his or her certification program must actively seek information while on the job; "I don't know" and ignorance of policies and the law is not the answer to special education dilemmas. A public school principal cannot rely solely on the special education director for assistance; he or she must be able to make and manage directives independently. Public school principals who lack knowledge and training can craft decisions affecting multiple members in the district. An inadequately prepared principal may be the one to dictate that the special education department "raise the bar"; the department is not only expected to get students back on grade level but to potentially excel beyond their capacity. When it comes to special education, public school principals may not realize how much they do not know.

Special education has been evolving for 35 years and will continue to do so; establishing a special education competency for public school principals will ensure principals of tomorrow are prepared today. The suggestion should be made that current certificate holders seeking employment complete training in special education as part of their induction program/process. Public school principals are required to promote successful learning for all students; understanding special education will make this goal and inclusion attainable. The public school principal must be knowledgeable regarding special education law and procedures (Billingsley, 2004; Crockett, 2002). The public school principal has multiple duties; to be an effective leader, principals should focus on improving professional skills and knowledge of the faculty and staff they lead and support (Billingsley, 2004; Crockett, 2002; DiPaola, Tschannen-Moran, &Walther-Thomas, 2004; NPBEA, 2015).

Conclusion

Public school principals are not only leaders of the school, they are instructional leaders for all (Darling-Hammond et al., 2007). Public school principals are the most influential individuals in a district; they ensure high-quality education, and teaching happens consistently throughout the building they supervise (Darling-Hammond et al., 2007); this includes special education. To be considered an instructional leader, a public school principal "must be knowledgeable about evidence-based practices within the field of both general and special education" (Pazey & Cole, 2012, p. 258). As mandated by law, public schools have the responsibility to identify students with learning and behavior deficits to enable them to receive supports needed to be academically successful.

Instructional leadership is essentially anything the public school principal can do to foster and enhance learning and teaching for all students. What subgroup in any school district across the country needs more enhanced learning and specialized teaching than those served by special education? Today's public school principals should commit to discovering ways to boost the achievement of the special education population. Public school principals should have the desire to be actively involved in special education; whether they are a facilitator or the team leader, principals must remain informed. One of the first steps to becoming a better instructional leader is to develop self-awareness. When talking about public education, public school principals must be aware their knowledge is lacking. Public school principals should desire to fill their knowledge gaps and develop a solid understanding of IDEA, the history behind special education, and how one decision can affect many.

What is the educational impact? To produce qualified staff who are ready to be the instructional leaders of any building they enter, public school principal training programs must add a special education competency to their certification process to eliminate the lack of knowledge many new principals have. Mandating one class be taken to achieve proficiency in special education is not enough. Stringent universal coursework should be added to address special education topics and initiatives. A principal who has a solid understanding of special education procedures, IDEA, and the school code is more likely going to have a special education staff who is supportive and in favor of their directives. They will have staff wanting to be actively involved in curriculum planning, developing policy change, and striving for professional excellence. If the leader of the school does not have the proper knowledge of special education law and policy, it does not garner adequate respect and trust from special education staff, as decisions can be called into question due to lack of understanding. Having special education background knowledge will enable public school principals to understand the IEP process, empowering them to help make and support IEP team decisions as they arise. Requiring public school principals to complete more training in special education will not only make them more well-rounded professionally, it adds credibility to their decisions involving special education policies and students. Knowledge is power.

Some public school principals fear due process; having a public school principal who is knowledgeable in special education law and procedure will make the IEP team a more cohesive unit. Members of each public school district must work together to bring about positive change in the lives of their students and boost academic achievement. The public school principal must have the influence over his or her faculty/staff to motivate all parties toward the common goal. A good leader will seek information from all team members; he or she will bring about positive change by asking for input from all; developing/implementing new policies/procedures, and curriculum; and continuously striving to improve morale and work performance.

There is no question special education knowledge is lacking in public school principal training degrees and programs. To combat this lack of knowledge, special education competency needs to be a mandatory component in public school principal preparation training programs. The suggestion should be made that current certificate holders seeking employment must complete training in special education as part of their induction program/process, and yearly special education professional development should also be completed. Public school principals are required to promote successful learning for all students; understanding special education will make this goal attainable. Special education has been evolving for 35 years and will continue to do so; having a solid foundation in special education will ensure the nation's instructional leaders of tomorrow are prepared today.

References

Angelle, P., & Bilton, L. M. (2009). Confronting the unknown: Principal preparation training in issues related to special education. *AASA Journal of Scholarship & Practice, 5*(4), 5–9.

Ball, K., & Green, R. L. (2014). An investigation of the attitudes of school leaders toward the inclusion of students with disabilities in the general education setting. *National Forum of Applied Educational Research Journal, 27*(1/2), 57–76.

Bargerhuff, M. E. (2001). Inclusive elementary schools and those who lead them. *Electronic Journal for Inclusive Education, 1*(5). Retrieved from http://corescholar.libraries.wright.edu/cgi/viewcontent.cgi?article=1030&context=ejie

Bateman, D., & Bateman, C. F. (2001). *A principal's guide to special education.* Arlington, VA: Council for Exceptional Children.

Bays, D. A., & Crockett, J. B. (2007). Investigating instructional leadership for special education. *Exceptionality, 15*(3), 143–161. doi:10.1080/09362830701503495

Billingsley, B. S. (2004). Promoting teacher quality and retention in special education. *Journal of Learning Disabilities, 37*(5), 370–376.

Bon, S. C., & Bigbee, A. J. (2011). Special education leadership: Integrating professional and personal codes of ethics to serve the best interests of the child. *Journal of School Leadership, 21*(3) 324–359.

Carpenter, W. (2008). The other side of inclusion. *Educational Horizons, 86* (3).

Christensen, J., Robertson, J. S., Williamson, R., & Hunter, W. C. (2013). Preparing educational leaders for special education success: Principals' perspective. *The Researcher, 25*(1), 94–107.

Crockett, J. B. (2002). Special educations role in preparing responsive leaders for inclusive schools. *Remedial and Special Education, 23*(3), 157–168. doi:10.1177/07419325020230030401

Crum, K. S., Sherman, W. H., & Myran, S. (2010). Best practices of successful elementary school leaders. *Journal of Educational Administration, 48*(1), 48–63. doi:10.1108/09578231011015412

Cruzeiro, P. A., & Morgan, R. L. (2006). The rural principal's role with consideration for special education. *Education*, 126(3), 569–579.

Darling-Hammond, L., LaPointe, M., Meyerson, D., Orr. M. T., & Cohen, C. (2007). *Preparing school leaders for a changing world: Lessons from exemplary leadership development programs.* Stanford, CA: Stanford University, Stanford Educational Leadership Institute.

Davis, W. E. (1980). An analysis of principal's formal training in special education. *Education*, 101(1), 89–94.

DiPaola, M., & Walther-Thomas, C. (2003). *Principals and special education: The critical role of school leaders* (COPPSE document no. Ib-7). Gainsville: University of Florida, Center on Personnel Studies in Special Education.

DiPaola, M., Tschannen-Moran, M., & Walther-Thomas, C. (2004). School principals and special education: Creating the context for academic success. *Focus on Exceptional Children, 37*(1), 1–10.

Downing, J. E., & Peckham-Hardin, K. D. (2007). Inclusive education: What makes it a good education for students with moderate to severe disabilities? *Research and Practice for Persons with Severe Disabilities, 32*(1), 16–30. doi:10.2511/rpsd.32.1.16

Frick, W. C., & Faircloth, S. C. (2007). Acting in the collective and individual "best interests of students": When ethical imperatives clash with administrative demands. *Journal of Special Education Leadership, 20*(1), 21–32.

Frost, L. A., & Kersten, T. (2011). The role of the elementary principal in the instructional leadership of special education. *International Journal of Educational Leadership Preparation, 6*(2). Retrieved from http://files.eric.ed.gov/fulltext/EJ973829.pdf

Garrison-Wade, D., Sobel, D., & Fulmer, C. L. (2007). Inclusive leadership: Preparing principals for the role that awaits them. *Educational Leadership & Administration, 19*, 117–132.

Hallahan, D. P., Kauffman, J. M., & Pullen, P. C. (2015). Exceptional learners: An introduction to special education (13th ed.). Boston, MA: Pearson.

Heward, W. L. (2000). *Exceptional children: An introduction to special education* (6th ed.). Upper Saddle River, NJ: Prentice Hall.

Individuals with Disabilities Education Act Amendments of 1997 (IDEA.) (2004). Retrieved from http://uscode.house.gov/statutes/pl/94/142.pdf

Katsiyannis, A., Losinski, M., & T. Prince, A. M. (2012). Litigation and students with disabilities: A persistent concern. *NASSP Bulletin, 96*(1), 23–43. doi:10.1177/0192636511431008

Lasky, B., & Karge, B. D. (2006). Meeting the needs of students with disabilities: Experience and confidence of principals. *NASSP Bulletin, 90*(1), 19–36.

Lynch, J. M. (2012). Responsibilities of today's principal: Implications for principal preparation programs and principal certification policies. *Rural Special Education Quarterly, 31*(2), 40–47.

Mackenna, L. (2017, March 23). How a New Supreme Court Ruling Could Affect Special Education. The Atlantic. Retrieved July 30, 2018, from https://www.theatlantic.com/education/archive/2017/03/how-a-new-supreme-court-ruling-could-affect-special-education/520662/

McLeskey, J., Landers, E., Williamson, P., & Hoppey, D. (2012). Are we moving toward educating students with disabilities in less restrictive settings? *Journal of Special Education, 46*(3), 131–140. doi:10.1177/0022466910376670

McHatton, P. A., Boyer, N. R., Shaunessy, E., & Terry, P. M. (2010). Principals' perceptions of preparation and practice in gifted and special education content: Are we doing enough? *Journal of Research on Leadership Education, 5*(1), 1–22.

Miller, C. M., & Martin, B. N. (2014). Principal preparedness for leading in demographically changing schools. *Educational Management Administration & Leadership, 43*(1), 129–151. doi:10.1177/1741143213513185

National Policy Board for Educational Administration. (2015). *Professional standards for educational leaders 2015*. Reston, VA: Author.

No Child Left Behind (NCLB) Act of 2001, Pub. L. No. 107–110, § 115, Stat. 1425 (2002).

Pazey, B. L., & Cole, H. A. (2013). The role of special education training in the development of socially just leaders. *Educational Administration Quarterly, 49*(2), 243–271. doi:10.1177/0013161x12463934

Reames, E. (2010). Shifting paradigms: Redesigning a principal preparation programs' curriculum. *Journal of Research on Leadership Education, 5*(12), 436–459. doi:10.1177/194277511000501205

Sage, D. D., & Burrello, L. C. (1994). Leadership in educational reform: An administrator's guide to changes in special education. Baltimore, MD: P.H. Brookes.

Taylor-Backor, K. & Gordon, S. (2015). Preparing principals as instructional leaders: Perceptions of university faculty, expert principals, and expert teacher leaders. NASSP Bulletin. 99. 10.1177/0192636515587353.

Tubbs, J. E., Heard, M. S., & Epps, A. (2011). Principals preparation program: Managing the learning environment using ELCC standards. *Contemporary Issues in Education Research (CIER), 4*(4), 17–24. doi:10.19030/cier.v4i4.4164

Voltz, D. L., & Collins, L. (2010). Preparing special education administrators for inclusion in diverse, standards-based contexts: Beyond the Council for Exceptional Children and the Interstate School Leaders Licensure Consortium. *Teacher Education and Special Education, 33*(1), 70–82.

Wakeman, S., Browder, D., Flowers, C., & Ahlgrim-Delzell, L. (2006). Principals' knowledge of fundamental and current issues in special education, *NASSP Bulletin, 90*(2), 153–174.

Wright, P. W., & Wright, P. D. (2007). *Wrightslaw: Special education law* (2nd ed.). Hartfield, VI: Hartfield House Law Press.

Yell, M. L. (2016). The law and special education (4th ed.). Boston, MA: Pearson.

Zirkel, P. A. (2012). Case law under the IDEA: 1998 to the present. In *IDEA: A handy desk reference to the law, regulations, and indicators* (pp. 669–752). Albany, NY: Lexis-Nexis.

Zirkel, P. (2013). Adjudicative remedies for denials of FAPE under the IDEA. *Journal of National Association of Administrative Law Judiciary, 33*(1), 220–241.

Zirkel, P. (2016). Parental participation: The paramount procedural requirement under the IDEA? *Connecticut Public Interest Law Journal, 15*(1), 1–36.

Zirkel, P. (2017). Endrew F. after six months: A game changer? *West's Education Law Reporter, 348,* 585–596.

EXTENSION ACTIVITIES

Discussion Questions

1. The issue at hand is whether public school principals are adequately prepared to lead special education once they are certified. Angelle and Bilton (2009), Davis (1980), Lasky and Karge (2006), Lynch (2012), McHatton, Boyer, Shaunessy and Terry (2013), and Pazey and Cole (2013) have all noted the discrepancy between principal preparation programs and subsequent practice. Many certification programs only require one class designated toward special education in their programming, while others do not have any.

   a. Design a sample course syllabus for a principal certification class to increase the special education knowledge of its participants.

   b. What are the most critical areas you feel public school principals should be trained in to successfully lead special education programming?

   c. What different types of projects would you design to demonstrate competency in areas you targeted as critical competencies and skills?

   d. How can state departments of education and certification programs ensure public school principal training programs are providing relevant on-the-job information for candidates?

2. Create a timeline of landmark court cases and events you feel public school principals should be aware of to adequately make special education decisions. Make sure your timeline includes dates and information pertinent to special education leadership.

3. If state-level departments of education are unwilling to change certification requirements for individuals to become certified principals, what can school districts do to ensure their leaders are prepared to handle special education dilemmas? How does a school board determine whether a candidate for a public school principal leadership position is qualified to lead a special education department, let alone an entire building? Explain your answer and use research to corroborate your position. Be sure to include properly cited APA in-text citations (when appropriate) from any supporting evidence used.

4. Review the requirements for individuals to become a certified public school principal in your state. Pick five universities/colleges in the state you have chosen and review the credit load, coursework, and curriculum requirements to obtain the degree/certificate. What commonalities do you observe? What differences? Was there a special education component? Would you make any suggestions based on what you have read to improve their program? Be sure to include properly cited APA in-text citations (when appropriate) from any supporting evidence used.

5. Zirkel (2013) completed a review of 224 court decisions to look for trends in special education cases. Out of the cases reviewed, states with the highest FAPE violations were "(1) New York—thirty-five (16%); (2) California—thirty-two (14%); (3) Hawaii—twenty-two (10%); (4) Pennsylvania—nineteen (8%); (5) New Jersey—thirteen (6%); (6) Texas—eleven (5%); and (7) Alaska—ten (4%)" (Zirkel, 2013, p. 226). Examine the ODR website for due process hearings in your area and complete a case study. Identify the following:

   a. What is the primary disability of the student who was involved in the hearing?
   b. What is the primary issue? (FAPE, LRE, SDI, etc.) Is there more than one issue?
   c. Provide a chronological summary of the major facts in the case, identifying key elements that occurred, which resulted in the parent filing due process proceedings.
   d. What previous case law was cited to provide a foundation/grounds for the case in question?
   e. If you were the public school principal of the district in question, what, if anything, could have been done to avoid due process proceedings?

Write a Letter Assignment

Pick a side:

> The research has demonstrated that, overall, public school principals receive little to no formal training in leading special education in their degree and/or certification programs. Write a proposal to the Department of Education citing the reasons why special education training should be a mandatory component for all principal certification programs.

> Write a proposal to the Department of Education citing the reasons why public school principal certification and education training should programs should remain status quo.

Discussion Paper

After reading this chapter, find a minimum of two additional articles that support this topic and write a double-spaced discussion paper following APA guidelines, including a bibliography page, to address the following:

- Before reading this chapter, my opinion on this issue was _____.

- In your own words, what is the issue at hand?

- Analyze what you see as the two sides of this issue.

- Identify a perceived misconception from either side. (When doing this, list the actual sentence(s) or portion of the sentence, citing the page number that you are making reference to, then write your response as to why you think it is a misconception. The key word is "perceived.")

- And finally, which side do you personally agree with more and why? (Refer to your personal experiences, here. If you have dealt with this issue in your personal life, work, teaching, etc., include that information in your answer.)

- Make sure to include in-text citations (when appropriate) from the supporting articles that you found.

Chapter 16

Disciplinary Procedures
What Considerations Should be Made for Students
With Special Needs?

Mark D. Hogue and Jeffrey D. Keeling

PICTURE THIS: One day after stating that he wants to harm one of his classmates, Billy, a ninth grader who receives services for a specific learning disability in reading as well as itinerant emotional support services, is found to be in possession of a two-inch folding pocket knife. During a meeting with the principal, Billy justifies his possession of the knife by stating that he feels threatened by Joe, a fellow ninth grader whose locker is adjacent to Billy's. According to Billy, Joe has been saying that he is going to "punch Billy in the face if he makes that annoying train whistle noise again." Billy's school, Excelsior Jr./Sr. High, has a zero-tolerance policy regarding weapons in all forms, including knives. According to the policy, any student who uses or possesses a weapon on school property will face expulsion from school for up to one calendar year. Given Billy's status as a student with special needs, how should the principal proceed in a manner compliant with special education law and the school district's policy?

What Is the Issue?

A prevailing misconception held by many individuals, students, parents, and even school employees is that Billy, a student with a special needs diagnosis, has carte blanche in a situation such as the one described; that is, Billy has been insulated by virtue of his IEP and traditional disciplinary consequences do not apply to him. This perspective represents a significant misinterpretation of the procedural safeguards ensured by the Individuals with Disabilities Education Act (IDEA).

IDEA contains a series of procedural safeguards focused on ensuring that students with special needs are not removed from their least restrictive environment (LRE) without appropriate cause. Ultimately, IDEA guarantees every student with special needs requiring special education services the right to a free and appropriate public education (FAPE). No language exists in IDEA stating that a student with special needs is free from school-based disciplinary action as outlined in the student-parent handbook and governed by the local education agency (LEA). In keeping with the spirit of FAPE, appropriate discipline arguably is an important element of a holistic educational experience. As such, failure to address serious and dangerous school (and potentially legal) infractions through the LEA's policies would, in and of itself, constitute an injustice to the student with special needs. By implementing the proper corrective action in accordance with applicable laws, school and district leaders can take a significant step toward preventing similar transgressions in the future.

As stated in the opening vignette, the school that Billy attends has taken a harsh stance against the possession of weapons on school property. The notion of "zero tolerance" is arguably the most pervasive discipline reform effort across American public schools over the past 25 years, with the primary focus centering around weapons (Gregory & Cornell, 2009). While zero-tolerance policies are well intentioned in their goal of imposing stringent consequences on those who violate their stated rules, such policies pose to be equally problematic in cases involving students with special needs receiving special education services (American Psychological Association (APA) Zero Tolerance Task Force, 2006).

In addition to empowering parents in the educational process, one of the charter precepts of IDEA is that students identified as having special needs are ensured FAPE. All students with special needs receiving special education services have undergone a rigorous identification process that involves a battery of cognitive assessments in addition to psychological and medical evaluations in certain cases. Following the evaluation, a student is determined to have qualified or not qualified for special education services in accordance with pre-defined standardized measures. If a student meets the qualifications for special education services, a multi-disciplinary team (MDT), including relevant teachers, administrators, the child's parents/guardians, and, if age 14 or older, the student, convenes to develop an individualized educational plan (IEP) for the child.

The purpose of the IEP is to ensure that the child's program of studies adheres to the tenets of FAPE (Fan, 2014). As such, investigating and pursuing the role and appropriateness of discipline is required—in keeping with due process rights—to follow a process for all students beyond school-level discipline. To clarify, any student who is suspended for a period greater than or equal to 3 days is guaranteed the right to an informal hearing with members of the district administrative team. However, when disciplinary matters transcend a primary level of consequence, students with special needs are entitled to additional safeguards related to the enactment of an extended suspension. Thus, immediately moving to expel a student with Billy's special needs represents a change in his educational placement that may not be aligned with the provisions set forth in the IEP and is inconsistent with the student's due process rights as protected by IDEA.

While any suspension from school activities represents a minor change of placement, a suspension or expulsion beyond 10 days constitutes a significant change in placement. As is the case with all students, those with special needs can be suspended for up to 10 days.

However, students with special needs have unique rights if the corrective action identified by a school district aims to suspend or expel them for more than 10 days. Expulsion and suspensions over 10 days are considered a change in placement for students with special needs and therefore require strict protocols in order to ensure that the best interest of the student is preserved.

In fact, the notion of resting on a school policy such as "zero tolerance" or "automatic expulsion" stands in stark contrast to IDEA. To this end, traditional expulsions are no longer permitted for students with special needs, even in the case of weapons violations. Again, the focus is squarely centered on the student through the procedural safeguards outlined by IDEA.

Further, it is of principle concern that the student's action of bringing a weapon into the school could be a direct result of the student's identified disabilities. As a result, well in advance of a full 10-day suspension pending possible expulsion, the multi-disciplinary team (MDT) must reconvene to hold a manifestation determination meeting as outlined in IDEA. The goal of this meeting is focused singularly on identifying whether the behavior that led to the disciplinary infraction represents a preponderant "manifestation" of the child's disability (Turnbull, 2009). Under IDEA, the manifestation determination is, indeed, a process. The manifestation determination process should be individualized and unique in each circumstance; it should never be grossly minimized to asking if the student with special needs knows the difference between right and wrong. According to Dwyer (1996), "[A] manifestation determination must include an analysis of the child's program as well as the child's physical, cognitive, developmental, mental, and emotional challenges … these factors must be viewed in the context of ecological variables and IEP services and goals" (p. 7).

If the MDT determines that the child's behavior is a direct result of his or her identified disabilities, then the possibility of expulsion no longer exists. Similarly, even though a student with special needs cannot be expelled for a behavior deemed as a manifestation of his or her disability, it also does not mean that the student will remain in his or her current placement. After a significant disciplinary infraction, 45-day placements are a common recommendation by the MDT for students with special needs following a manifestation determination meeting. In summary, while the student is not technically expelled for the 45-day period, the behavior (e.g., weapons, drugs, and/or significant bodily harm) represents the most significant and concerning level of conduct and is justifiable grounds for the MDT to insist on the student's placement/enrollment in an interim alternative education setting (IAES). It is important to note that this 45-day alternative placement may occur with or without the agreement of the student's parents/guardians.

All weapons violations in public schools are required to be reported to local law enforcement. This can lead to legal charges for the student in question; however, these proceedings are largely left to the juvenile or criminal justice systems to assess and address. School personnel, including teachers and administrators, may be called on to testify in court if a case reaches the level of being heard by a judge. From a principal's perspective, it is critical that all aspects of the process are documented meticulously and readily available in the event that they are needed in the future. This documentation should encompass the corpus of all factual evidence from the proceedings, including relevant data from the event, a written narrative of the event, witness and victim statements, and other relevant artifacts such as security camera footage. Please refer to figure 16.1, which outlines the disciplinary process for students with special needs.

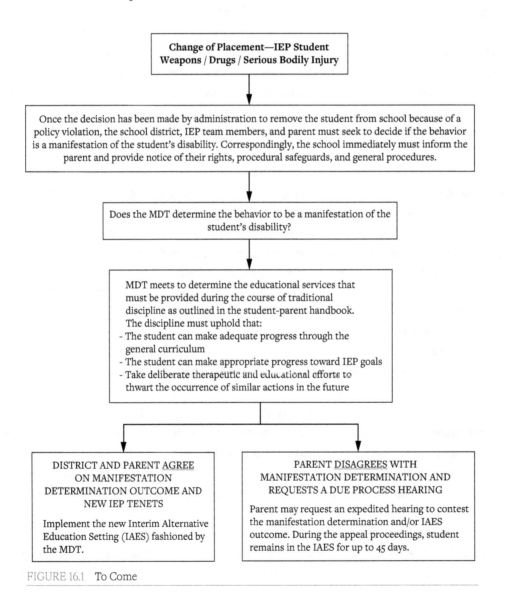

FIGURE 16.1   To Come

If the behavior, in this case possessing a knife, is determined not to be a manifestation of the child's behavior, then the school district may proceed with the expulsion process; however, there is a caveat. If the school district goes through the expulsion proceedings and ultimately rules to expel the student with special needs, the district is not only required to play a direct role in securing a more appropriate educational placement for the student, but also is responsible to pay for and oversee the child's education in the placement determined by the MDT. While individual circumstances most assuredly dictate the cost to educate specific students with special needs (e.g., placement cost, transportation needs, support staff, etc.), it is not uncommon that an expulsion of a student with an IEP may cost a school district tens of thousands of dollars. The cost of educating students out of district can take a significant toll on a district's fund balance.

By their very nature, and especially in light of the school violence epidemic, weapons violations have the potential to elicit widespread concern among parents and the news media. As such, it is the primary responsibility of the school system to ensure that the health, safety, and welfare of all students are protected. Ironically, school districts often are prevented from sharing details about weapons violations with the public as a result of confidentiality laws, which apply to the policy violator just as they apply to all students. This can result in a misconception on the part of the public that "nothing is being done" by schools. Regardless of the potential for public backlash resulting from the limited information that may be shared, school leaders, teachers, and other involved personnel must ensure that the privacy of all individuals involved with an incident is preserved.

What Does the Law Say?

From a legal perspective, all students possess due process rights when faced with allegations that could lead to an extended suspension or expulsion from school. All students are limited to 10 consecutive days of suspension from school without expulsion proceedings being initiated. In keeping with due process rights, within 3 days of the initiation of expulsion proceedings, students must be granted an informal hearing with the building principal in order to fully understand the charges against them and to provide any evidence to the contrary. It is both advisable and highly recommended that in cases involving disciplinary action against students with special needs that the school district's director or coordinator of special education services play an active role in the meeting. After the informal hearing, students also have the right to a hearing with the superintendent of schools in order to present their case. The superintendent maintains the sole discretion to move toward expulsion proceedings or to recommend an alternative. In the vast majority of cases involving students with special needs, the superintendent will recommend an alternative to expulsion.

Given the litigious nature of the society in which we live, the full investigation of all disciplinary incidents by school administrators is critical. Building principals especially must ensure that they have the clearest possible understanding of the circumstances surrounding the incident including witness testimony, any security camera footage, and relevant police reports. Further, the building principal must document all details and conversations related to the situation in exhaustive detail and maintain a file of information to be used in the event that the proceedings are called into question by parents/guardians or their legal representatives. School districts must operate with extreme caution when dealing with the discipline of students with special needs. Proceeding with caution will help school districts ensure that students' needs are addressed appropriately and will avoid placing themselves at risk for legal actions that could cost copious amounts of money and valuable time.

With this in mind, school administrators must be aware that even one day removed from the learning environment set forth in the IEP constitutes a change of educational placement, which, if not handled appropriately, could give parents reason to pursue legal challenges against the school district. Further, even if a school district opts to "expel" a student with special needs, the end result typically becomes a change of educational placement through the signing of a new notice of recommended educational placement (NOREP) by the child's parent or legal guardian. Again, in all cases of disciplinary changes of placement for students with special needs, the school district is responsible for bearing the full costs of tuition, transportation, and related services that the MDT believes are necessary for the student to be successful (Mancuso, Stotland, Reiser, & Pennsylvania Education Law Center, 2000).

One of the key components of IDEA is the requirement that students with special needs be placed in the least restrictive environment (LRE). This simply means that students with special needs must be educated in a setting that is as close as possible to that in which their peers receiving regular education are enrolled. The right to education in the least restrictive environment is not forfeited when a student with special needs is found to be guilty of committing a disciplinary infraction. When the MDT meets to discuss changes to a student's educational placement resulting from disciplinary issues, the team must be careful to ensure that any and all alternative placements are not more restrictive than necessary in addressing the student's specific needs.

In the years prior to IDEA, students with special needs who violated district policies were often sent to placements with little regard for whether they best met the needs of the individual. The benefit of IDEA is that it ensures the right to a free and appropriate education for students with special needs. Operating within these guidelines can be challenging for school districts given seemingly chronic funding issues and a lack of appropriate alternative placements for students with special needs, particularly in more remote rural areas. In spite of these challenges, school districts must maintain the best interest of students as their highest priority while ensuring that all appropriate legal procedures are followed and carried out.

How Does This Affect Schools?

Disciplinary matters involving students with special needs have the potential to be both time consuming and costly for school districts. Therefore, it is imperative that legally vetted procedures are outlined and in place in order for district administrators to avoid making momentary decisions that violate the provisions of IDEA or other relevant special education laws. As discussed previously, the appropriate documentation of all aspects and information surrounding the incident in question is of paramount importance. Appropriate investigation and subsequent documentation represent a critical component in the process of ensuring that both the affected student(s) and the school district are kept in the best possible legal position.

When dealing with disciplinary matters, school districts must also rely on past precedent in order to ensure that the resulting actions represent as high of a degree of "fairness" as possible. One of the primary issues that schools face when handling these matters is the discrepancy that occurs when a student receiving regular education services and a student with special needs are guilty of the same infraction. In the previously discussed scenario involving the knife in school, a regular education student undoubtedly would have been expelled per the zero-tolerance policy. This, however, may not be the case for a student with special needs given the legalities related to the findings of the manifestation determination and the resulting changes in educational placement. As much of the general public is not aware of the intricacies of special education law, the potential for accusations of double standards on the part of the school exists. Further complicating matters is the fact that as a result of confidentiality laws such as the Family Educational Rights and Privacy Act (FERPA), limited information related to students in schools can be shared with the general public. This has the potential to leave school officials in the position of not being able to legally address questions, which can result in unrest on the part of the general public.

For example, in the case of Billy and Joe, as outlined in the opening vignette, the school administrator involved would be well served to contact Joe's parents and inform them of the general circumstances of the incident. The administrator also should explain that he or she is legally unable to provide details related to the discipline of another student (e.g., Billy). During the conversation with the parents, the administrator should focus solely on the facts related to the incident as they apply to their specific child and avoid discussing outcomes related to the discipline of any other students.

Another challenge when working through matters of discipline involving students with special needs is ensuring that students' parents or guardians will follow through with the recommendations developed by the MDT. School districts can follow all applicable laws and have the absolute best intentions in providing a quality educational experience for students with special needs; however, many of these efforts can be thwarted if they are not supported effectively in the home. For this reason, parental involvement from the point at which a student is first identified as having special needs is critical. The more involved and informed parents and guardians are in the earlier phases of the educational process, the better qualified they will be to reinforce practices that are in the students' best interests on the home front.

Also worth noting is the fact that school district policies and law enforcement approaches may sometimes vary. For example, the school district may take a harsh stand against the possession of even a short knife blade, while the local law enforcement agency may state that it does not constitute a significant threat to public safety and file no charges. Similarly, a school district may not respond as severely to an incident involving social media bullying done outside of and unrelated to the school; however, local law enforcement personnel may likely consider filing harassment charges on the offending student. In these instances, it is critical that school personnel adhere to the policies adopted by their local school boards. Regardless of how other agencies react, all actions taken by the school district must be aligned with the policies adopted by the district's governing board.

Perhaps the most important piece of information that should be remembered is that the safety of students and staff members is the highest priority of school leaders. As such, a balance must be struck between ensuring that the rights of students with special needs are protected while also ensuring the safety of the remainder of the school's population. Therefore, if a student with special needs causes a threat to the safety of others, this must be factored into the MDT's discussion and subsequent recommendations following the incident. If a student is capable of conducting wide-reaching harm, regardless of identification as regular education or special education, he or she must be removed from the environment in order to ensure that the remaining student population is not placed in a high-risk situation. The removal of a student with special needs from a school district is a delicate process, and the rights of all students, including the one who has violated the rules, must be considered. However, school leaders must place general welfare and safety higher than all other priorities.

What Is the Impact on Students Needing Special Education or 504 Plan Services?

The primary responsibility of school administrators, as well as any professionals working with students with special needs, is to make all decisions with the students' best interest given the highest priority. Bearing this principle in mind, simply doling out disciplinary consequences without a plan for rehabilitation and long-term improvement is of little benefit to the student (Marshall, 1993). When engaging with students who have special needs, administrators must remember that their primary objective is not to punish but to educate. This concept becomes even more significant when working with students with special needs given the fact that although there are consequences for negative behaviors, the true goal and desired outcome is the learning and adoption of appropriate behaviors.

When addressing students with special needs during conferences or other settings, administrators must be aware of the specific disabilities possessed by the involved student or students. This means, for example, that if a student has English language comprehension difficulties, the administrator may need to call in a third party who works with the student regularly in order to promote understanding. Similarly, a student with severe emotional needs may require that the conversation be held in an area in which he or she feels secure as opposed to the harsher setting of the office.

Ultimately, students should leave a conference, held for the purpose of discussing behavioral concerns, feeling empowered to make positive changes in their decision-making processes as opposed to feeling dishonored and/or undignified. For this reason, school administrators must be acutely aware of the background of students who are being addressed for policy violations. Further, administrators must strive to build a solid rapport with the parents of students with special needs, as parental support can make or break a student's long-term success and rehabilitation following an infraction (Skiba & Rausch, 2006). If there is a general lack of follow-through on the part of parents, then attempting to bring about positive change solely from the side of the school becomes a nearly impossible task.

What Is the Impact on Students in General Education?

Beyond the challenge of explaining to students in general education why their special education peers may not always be treated in the same manner for similar behaviors, the culture of the school as it relates to promoting interaction between regular education and special education students is critical. School administrators should provide opportunities for interaction among students regardless of their identification. One example of this is a high school that houses a life skills classroom for students with significant special needs. During study halls, regular education students are permitted to sign up to assist in the life skills classroom with reading and other appropriate tasks. Similarly, students with disabilities are educated with their peers in the general education population in all core subjects that do not require individualized educational programming. This interaction builds a sense of rapport and understanding between general and special education populations and contributes to an overall positive climate in the school.

Developing a culture of appreciation and understanding also assists when a general education student and a student with special needs are involved in the same disciplinary incident but receive different consequences. While some general education students (and their parents) may equate differences in disciplinary outcomes among those who have or do not have IEPs to unjust treatment, the focus of an effective paradigm for student discipline should focus on individual accountability. To further emphasize this point, the potential for differences in consequences should not come as a surprise to students in a school culture that promotes understanding and awareness in addition to relationship building among all student populations.

Conclusion

The subject of disciplining students with special needs truly is extensive and complex. The critical factor for those working with students with special needs is to remember that nearly every nuance of the special education field is governed by a detailed set of laws and regulations. As a result, decisions that have the potential to impact the educational placement of a student with special needs must not be made rashly without considering the best interest of the student and all applicable laws and regulations.

Although it is a complex matter, the disciplinary process can play a significant role in the educational program of students with special needs not only by assisting in the character building process, but also in ensuring that the student's needs are being met. Often, the disciplinary process provides an opportunity for the student's IEP and related services to be reviewed, thus prompting conversations that result in decisions that benefit the child. It is important to note that not all school employees are experts in special education law. As a result, they should construct a personal professional network that includes individuals such as special education directors, teachers, and other experienced colleagues to provide guidance and insight during times at which disciplinary issues involving students with special needs arise.

References

American Psychological Association Zero Tolerance Task Force. (2006). *Are zero tolerance policies effective in the schools? An evidentiary review and recommendations.* Washington, DC: Author.

Dwyer, K. P. (1996). Disciplining students with disabilities. *National Association of School Psychologists.* Bethesda, MD: .

Gregory, A., & Cornell, D. (2009). "Tolerating" adolescent needs: Moving beyond zero tolerance policies in high school. *Theory Into Practice, 48*(2), 106–113.

Fan, D. (2014). No idea what the future holds: The retrospective evidence dilemma. *Columbia Law Review, 114*(6), 1503–1547.

Mancuso, E., Stotland, J. F., Rieser, L., & Pennsylvania Education Law Center. (2000). The right to special education in Pennsylvania: A guide for parents. Retrieved from https://www.disabilityrightspa.org/wp-content/uploads/2019/02/The-Right-to-Special-Education-in-Pennsylvania-2009-Edition-1.pdf

Marshall, K. (1993). Teachers and schools: What makes a difference: A principal's perspective. *Daedalus, 122*(1), 209–242.

Skiba, R. & Rausch, M. (2006). School disciplinary systems: Alternatives to suspension and expulsion. In G. G. Bear & K. M. Mike (Eds.), *Children's needs III: Development, prevention, and intervention.* Bethesda, MD:

Turnbull, H. (2009). Today's policy contexts for special education and students with specific learning disabilities. *Learning Disability Quarterly, 32*(1), 3–9.

EXTENSION ACTIVITIES

School Board Presentation

After going through an arduous disciplinary situation involving a policy violation by a student with special needs, the board of school directors has reached out to the district's administrative team regarding information related to receiving more information about school-level discipline for students with special needs. You have been asked by the board to prepare a 30-minute presentation to better inform them. Prepare (a) a Microsoft PowerPoint (or the equivalent) presentation and (b) a one-page handout to supplement your presentation to be used during your presentation to the board. In your presentation and handout, be sure to include the following:

- A brief historical overview of the topic

- A review of the legal parameters of the topic

- Considerations and challenges affecting schools

- Best practices for handling student disciplinary matters for students with special needs

- At least two examples, one that addresses significant (e.g., weapons, drugs, significant bodily harm) and one that addresses less severe (e.g., defiant behavior, insubordination) behavior and how these matters would be handled by the MDT through IDEA.

Letter to Parents

In an effort to better communicate with a timid parent population after several high-profile discipline situations occurring in your district involving students with special needs, the state's Division of Compliance Monitoring suggests that the district draft a letter to all parents who have a student with special needs describing the procedural safeguards that are in place for students facing disciplinary consequences.

From an administrator's point of view, draft a professional letter, not to exceed three pages in length, that provides a readable and comprehensive overview of the procedural safeguards that protect the best interest of students with special needs. While honoring the process elements of potential disciplinary infractions, please also ensure that your correspondence stands as a positive point of communication with the families in your district who have children with special needs.

Your letter also should include a separate, one-page handout with an annotated list of at least five Web links and three print resources that parents may reference for further information on the topic.

Policy Analysis

In an attempt to provide a more comprehensive and student-centered approach to school policy, the superintendent of the school where you work (or one where you might work in the future) has asked you to provide expert advisement on drafting a new policy document to accompany the current school board policy that outlines student discipline. Currently, no such policy exists. The name of the policy that you will propose should be entitled "Discipline for Students with Special Needs" and should encapsulate the procedural elements of IDEA and due process in a document fashioned to match the existing student discipline policy that will precede it in the school district policy manual.

(Note: School board policy documents can be found online for most school districts. You should find a school in your region that has a specific student discipline policy but does not have a separate written policy addressing students with special needs.)

Submit your proposed "Discipline for Students with Special Needs" policy as well as a copy of the student discipline policy on which you based your proposal.

Discussion Paper

After reading this chapter, find a minimum of two additional articles that support this topic and write a double-spaced discussion paper following APA guidelines, including a bibliography page, to address the following:

- Before reading this chapter, my opinion on this issue was _____.

- In your own words, what is the issue at hand?

- Analyze what you see as the two sides of this issue.

- Identify a perceived misconception from either side. (When doing this, list the actual sentence(s) or portion of the sentence, citing the page number that you are referencing, and then write your response as to why you think it is a misconception. The key word is "perceived.")

- And finally, which side do you personally agree with more and why? (Refer to your personal experiences, here. If you have dealt with this issue in your personal life, work, teaching, etc., include that information in your answer.)

- Make sure to include in-text citations (when appropriate) from the supporting articles that you found.

Section IX

Collaboration and Partnerships

Chapter 17

Family Engagement
How to Create an Inclusive School Community

Brian L. Danielson

PICTURE THIS: It's parent-pickup time at Mossy Grove Middle School. You and a small collection of parents stand outside the middle school waiting for the students to be released for the day. As the students storm out, they are all waving around a purple sheet of paper. You quickly learn that it's an informational note for families that describes a new family engagement plan; the school would like parents to become more actively involved their children's education—both in the planning and the instruction. Your group begins a discussion on the topic—some are excited about the opportunity to be more directly involved in their child's education and some are totally against it.

What Is the Issue?

A lack of family engagement in education is considered by teachers, practitioners, administrators, and the community to be one of the largest challenges facing public schools today (McQuiggan & Megra, 2017). Especially as students progress through grade levels, family engagement declines so dramatically that by the time they reach middle school it is nearly nonexistent (Henderson A., Mapp, Johnson, & Davies, 2007).

The research over the past 30 years has consistently confirmed the importance of the role that families play in the social, emotional, and academic development of children in the classroom and in life (Henderson & Mapp, A New Wave of Evidence: The Impact of School, Family, and Community Connections on Student Achievement, 2002). However, there remains considerable discussion in the field regarding the barriers that hinder family engagement in education and the best practices for creating meaningful, lasting partnerships between the schools, families, and the community.

When surveyed, parents said that some of the barriers that hinder their engagement include overly busy schedules at home, feeling uncomfortable when communicating with school officials and staff, a lack of expertise and resources when it comes to helping their child learn, and frustration with school policy that either can't be changed or is hard to understand. Some parents also pointed out that the only time they heard from the school was when there was a problem (Education Policy and Practice Department, 2008).

Another barrier that schools face is understanding the difference between family involvement and family engagement. According to Ferlazzo and Hammond (2009), family involvement is focused on telling, consisting primarily of one-way communication between schools and home using tools such as prerecorded phone calls, newsletters, or notes to home. These tools are important and can be effective at informing families of school initiatives, projects, and information on how they can pitch in. However, they don't provide much of an opportunity for dialogue—inviting families to be part of the planning and decision making surrounding their child's education. Family engagement, on the other hand, focuses on creating meaningful, two-way partnerships between schools and families that allow families to help with crafting their child's academic, social, and emotional development at school (Ferlazzo & Hammond, 2009). To help maximize student achievement, schools and teachers need to work together with families to overcome these barriers and develop strong family engagement programs.

What Does the Law Say?

In their recent policy statement titled "Family Engagement from the Early Years to the Early Grades," the U.S. Department of Health and Human Services (HSS) and the U.S. Department of Education (ED) define family engagement as "the systematic inclusion of families in activities and programs that promote children's development, learning, and wellness, including in the planning, development, and evaluation of such activities, programs, and systems" (U.S. Department of Health and Human Services and Education, 2016, p. 1). This definition affirms the importance of family engagement to the academic, social, and emotional development of children; by creating strong, nurturing relationships between parents and teachers, families can become active participants in their child's education.

To help guide schools and educators, the policy statement provides 10 research-based principles of effective family engagement. These include strategies such as developing trusting and respectful relationships between families and professionals, developing meaningful relationships with community partners that support families, and providing professional development for staff on approaches for enhancing family engagement.

While this recent policy statement from the HSS and ED does provide a renewed emphasis on the topic, family engagement has been a common theme that can be seen throughout educational law and policy since the 1960s. For example, the Head Start Act of 1965 (reauthorized in 2007) encourages parental engagement by welcoming parents and families to participate in adult and parent educational activities and to join in classroom learning activities and prioritizing family members for potential employment in Head Start programs.

One of the purposes of the Child Care and Development Block Grant (2014) is to encourage family engagement in all areas of development in child care environments. It also requires states to provide education to parents and families regarding the research and best practices on family engagement and their role in positive child development.

The Individuals with Disabilities Education Act (IDEA) of 2004 emphasizes the importance of supporting families in meeting the educational needs of their children and their participation in their children's education. For example, Part B of IDEA requires schools to include parents as active members of the individualized education plan (IEP) team and that parental engagement data be included in annual performance reports to be publicly disclosed. IDEA also requires the development of individualized family plans, which provide services to children with disabilities and their families and establishes state grant funds to assist with providing early intervention services for eligible children. It also requires that those services be provided within the family context and in ways that enhance their ability to meet their children's educational and developmental needs. IDEA also provides grant funding to set up resource and educational centers to help families learn more about the services available to their children.

The Elementary and Secondary Education Act of 1965 (ESEA) requires that all school districts that receive Title I funds have parental engagement policies in place that detail strategies, expectations, and desired outcomes for implementing meaningful family engagement programs. These policies are to include strategies for including parents and families in the district-wide planning and the development of family engagement activities that improve student achievement.

How Does This Affect Schools?

Although federal law emphasizes it, and over 30 years of research confirm its importance, barriers continue to remain for schools. They must determine ways to overcome issues with family engagement specific to their district. One way that schools can overcome these barriers is to develop a meaningful family engagement plan. Joyce Epstein (2002) and colleagues and the Colorado Department of Education offer a model that many schools have adopted to promote high levels of family engagement. This model includes six types of school-wide activities that focus on parenting, communication, volunteering, learning at home, decision making, and collaborating with the community. Following is a brief description of each type and how they might be implemented.

Parenting: The first type of family engagement focuses on helping develop positive parenting skills at home and in the community. This might include schools providing adult education and training programs for parents; supports and resources for families on health, nutrition, and behavior management; or the development of workshops and videos on positive parenting skills.

Communication: Epstein's second type of family engagement emphasizes the development of effective one- and two-way communication about school programs and student progress. This type of family engagement might include one-way communications such as school-to-home notebooks, automated phone messages, newsletters, or updated webpages. This type of family engagement might also includes two-way communications such parent-teacher conferences, phones calls to the home with good news, or language translation, when needed.

Volunteering: The third type of family engagement presented by Epstein focuses on the recruitment and organization of family members to help and support school programs. To do this, schools might develop a formal volunteer program with clear expectations and outcomes using input from teachers, family members, and community partners. Schools might also survey family members for new and creative ways to partner or volunteer. Some schools have even created resource centers on their campus where parent volunteers can meet, plan, and work together on volunteering initiatives.

Learning at home: Epstein's fourth type of family engagement explores ways to educate family members on how to make the most of learning opportunities at home. This might include the school offering informational sessions for family members on what skills and learning outcomes are required for their children for each subject at each grade. Some schools might also provide training workshops on strategies for making homework a more meaningful learning experience for children.

Decision making: This type of family engagement emphasizes the importance of creating parent leaders by including family members in school decision making. Schools who take advantage of this type of family engagement often have active parent-teacher organizations/associations and district-level committees where family input is valued and seriously considered when making school- and district-wide decisions on curriculum and instruction.

Collaborating with community: The sixth type of family engagement featured in Epstein's model focuses on organizing and coordinating resources in the community that can support families, teachers, and schools in meeting their goals. One common approach for schools is to link specific student learning skills and talents to activities sponsored by community partners. Being strategic in this way not only adds real-world relevance to learning, but it also is a chance for schools and students to give back to the community in ways that matter.

Studies have found that implementing strong family engagement plans that take advantage of family and community partnerships, such as Epstein's, often result in upgrades to school facilities, improved school leadership, higher-quality learning programs, new resources for improving curriculum, and new funding for family supports and resources (Henderson, Mapp, Johnson, & Davies, 2007). More recently, Westrich and Strobel (2013) found in their research of the Redwood Community Schools that a strong family engagement plan also had a positive impact on schools by decreasing teacher workload, decreasing behavioral issues, boosting staff morale, and increasing school unity.

What Is the Impact on Students Needing Special Education or 504 Plan Services?

In their research, Henderson and Berla (1994) found that the best indicator of a student's success in school is the family's ability to create a home environment that values learning, communicates realistic expectations for success, and becomes engaged in the learning process—at home, in school, and in the community. One population who is also positively impacted by high levels of family engagement is students needing special education.

As discussed earlier, there are many barriers that prevent schools and teachers from engaging family members in meaningful ways. Fortunately, federal law reflects the importance of family engagement and establishes requirements that help ensure students who need special education receive the appropriate educational supports and services—at school, at home, and in the community.

While family inclusion in the development of learning outcomes has shown to improve student achievement for all students, it is not required for all students. However, under IDEA, family engagement is required for students needing special education. For example, for students with an IEP, schools are required to include family members as part of the IEP team. This means that, at least once a year, these family members have the opportunity to participate in the evaluation of their child's progress, discuss new educational goals for future development, and help determine what special education services will be needed to help their child meet their educational goals.

What Is the Impact on Students in General Education?

The research over the past 30 years confirms the importance of the role that families play in the academic achievement of children in the classroom and in life. Regardless of their sociocultural or socioeconomic background, students with parents who are engaged in their learning "are more likely to: earn higher grades and test scores, and enroll in higher-level programs, be promoted, pass their classes, earn credits, attend school regularly, have better social skills, show improved behavior, and adapt well to school, graduate and go on to post-secondary education" (Henderson & Mapp, 2002, p. 7).

The research also shows the positive impacts of family engagement on general education students to include working harder on their academics, performing better on assignments, and engaging more deeply in school programming. Family engagement also positively impacts general educational student's emotional well-being, making them feel more motivated, fostering a sense of pride in their academic achievements, and feeling more supported in their learning (Westrich & Strobel, 2013).

Conclusion

In summary, the research has shown that family engagement is a key factor in the social, emotional, and academic success of all students, in school and in life. However, there are many barriers that prevent schools from creating meaningful, impactful partnerships between teachers, family members, and the community. While federal law provides mechanisms for fostering family engagement for students needing special education, and policy statements from the HSS and ED offer best practices, there are many opportunities missed due to internal and external barriers. Some of these barriers originate from home, such as busy family schedules, and some originate at school, such as teachers only communicating with parents when there is a problem. Regardless, the research shows that many of these barriers can be overcome when schools implement comprehensive family engagement plans, such as the model provided by Epstein. Students, teachers, parents, school administrators, and community partners need to work together to develop a meaningful family engagement plan that supports the social, emotional, and academic success of all students.

References

Education Policy and Practice Deaprtment. (2008). *Parent, family, community involvement in education.* Washington, DC: National Education Association.

Epstein, J. L., Sanders, M. G., Simon, B. S., Salinas, K. C., Jansorn, N. R., & Van Voorhis, F. L. (2002). *School, family, and community partnerships: Your handbook for action.* Thousand Oaks, CA: Corwin.

Ferlazzo, L., & Hammond, L. A. (2009). *Building parent engagement in schools.* Santa Barbara, CA: ABC-CLIO.

Henderson, A. T., & Berla, N. (1994). *A new generation of evidence: The family is critical.* Washington, DC: National Committee for Citizens in Education.

Henderson, A. T., & Mapp, K. L. (2002). *A new wave of evidence: The impact of school, family, and community connections on student achievement.* Austin, TX: National Center for Family and Community Connections with Schools.

Henderson, A., Mapp, K., Johnson, V., & Davies, D. (2007). *Beyond the bake sale: The essential guide to family-school partnerships.* New York, NY: New Press.

McQuiggan, M., & Megra, M. (2017). *Parent and family involvement in education: Results from the National Household Education Surveys Program of 2016.* Washington, DC: U.S. Department of Education.

U.S. Department of Education. (1965). *Law and guidance.* Retrieved from https://www2.ed.gov/policy/landing.jhtml?src=pn

U.S. Department of Education. (n.d.). *Individuals with Disabilities Education Act.* Retrieved from https://sites.ed.gov/idea/

U.S. Department of Heath and Human Services. (2007). Head Start policy and regulations. Head Start. Retrieved from https://eclkc.ohs.acf.hhs.gov/policy/head-start-act

U.S. Department of Health and Human Services. (2014). Child care and development fund reauthorization. *Office of Child Care.* Retrieved from https://www.acf.hhs.gov/occ/ccdf-reauthorization

U.S. Department of Health and Human Services and Education. (2016). *Policy statement on family engagement from the early years to the early grades.* Retrieved from https://www2.ed.gov/about/inits/ed/earlylearning/files/policy-statement-on-family-engagement.pdf

Westrich, L., & Strobel, K. (2013). *A study of family engagement in Redwood City community schools.* Stanford, CA: W. Gardner Center for Youth and their Communities.

EXTENSION ACTIVITIES

Discussion Questions

1. The research shows that both family involvement and family engagement are important and effective in their own rights.

a. Describe a situation when strategies for *family involvement* would be more appropriate than strategies for family engagement.

b. Describe a situation when strategies for *family engagement* would be more appropriate than strategies for family involvement.

2. Family involvement and family engagement are often used synonymously, and most schools do both. However, there is a distinction. Reflect on how you and your school approach family interaction. Does your school do more telling or listening?

a. What strategies do you use to promote *family involvement?*

b. What strategies do you use to promote *family engagement?*

c. What steps can you take to move your school toward strategies that promote more *family engagement?*

3. There are many barriers that hinder schools and teachers from developing meaningful and lasting family relationships.

a. Describe what barriers you, as a teacher, have experienced and the steps have you taken (or might take) to overcome those barriers.

b. From your perspective, describe any barriers that your school might be facing and what might be done.

Write a Letter Assignment

Pick a side:

> Write a letter from a parent's perspective to the school administrator outlining the reasons why you are not more fully engaged in your child's learning at school, at home, and in the community.

> Write a letter from a parent's perspective to the school administrator asking why there are not more opportunities to engage in your child's education, including specific ideas on how you would like to be more engaged.

Discussion Paper

After reading this chapter, find a minimum of two additional articles that support this topic and write a double-spaced discussion paper following APA guidelines, including a bibliography page, to address the following:

- Before reading this chapter, my opinion on this issue was _____.

- In your own words, what is the issue at hand?

- Analyze what you see as the two sides of this issue.

- Identify a perceived misconception from either side. (When doing this, list the actual sentence(s) or portion of the sentence, citing the page number that you are making reference to, then write your response as to why you think it is a misconception. The key word is "perceived.")

- And finally, which side do you personally agree with more and why? (Refer to your personal experiences, here. If you have dealt with this issue in your personal life, work, teaching, etc., include that information in your answer.)

- Make sure to include in-text citations (when appropriate) from the supporting articles that you found.